basic PROJECTS

Visual Basic

2008

> John Giles

www.payne-gallway.co.uk

✓ Free online support
✓ Useful weblinks
✓ 24 hour online ordering

01865 888070

PAYNE-GALLWAY
Part of Pearson

Payne-Gallway is an imprint of Pearson Education Limited, a company incorporated in England and Wales, having its registered office at Edinburgh Gate, Harlow, Essex, CM20 2JE. Registered company number: 872828

www.payne-gallway.co.uk

Text © David Waller 2009

First published 2009

13 12 11 10 09
10 9 8 7 6 5 4 3 2 1

British Library Cataloguing in Publication Data
A catalogue record for this book is available from the British Library.

ISBN 978 1 905292 59 2

Designed by Wooden Ark Studios
Edited and typeset by Sparks – www.sparkspublishing.com
Cover design by Wooden Ark Studios
Printed in the UK by Scotprint

Acknowledgements
Every effort has been made to contact copyright holders of material reproduced in this book. Any omissions will be rectified in subsequent printings if notice is given to the publishers.

Websites
The websites used in this book were correct and up-to-date at the time of publication. It is essential for tutors to preview each website before using it in class so as to ensure that the URL is still accurate, relevant and appropriate. We suggest that tutors bookmark useful websites and consider enabling students to access them through the school/college intranet.

Ordering Information
Payne-Gallway, FREEPOST (OF1771),
PO Box 381, Oxford OX2 8BR
Tel: 01865 888070
Fax: 01865 314029
Email: orders@payne-gallway.co.uk

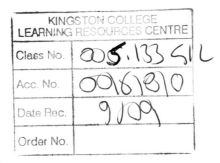

CONTENTS

So you know ...

Visual Basic is a program that you can use to make your own programs; you could start with some of the ideas in this book and, if you are keen, you could even make your own games. This process of producing new programs is called **programming** and can be a very rewarding pastime or career, so it is a good idea to get some experience and see if you like it: this is where this book can help!

Computer programming is done by writing **code**, which is a similar process to writing a secret code to prevent others from reading your private letters – something that you may have done already. There are many different ways of making a secret code and this is also true in programming: we call these **programming languages**. The **Basic** language is one of the most commonly used programming languages and within it there are various forms of the language; we are going to use **Visual Basic** (often just called **VB**), which has the advantage of being able to produce programs that look professional without relying on a great deal of programming experience. If you are bitten by the programming bug, you could download the free version (**Microsoft Visual Basic 2008 Express Edition**), which is the one referred to in this book.

Working through the activity in the introduction will help you to become familiar with the VB software by showing you some of the basic functionality.

This book also helps you to develop your functional skills in ICT. This is all about you being able to use your software skills in the way that best suits the activity that you have been given – in other words *why* you are doing something in the way that you have chosen. For example, you need to always be thinking about the purpose of what you are doing – what has it got to do with the project, what kind of impact do you want to achieve, who is going to see or use what you're working on i.e. who is your audience, and what is the background of the situation – for example, do you need to produce a formal or informal document? By considering all of these things you should be able to produce the right kind of documents which are 'fit for purpose', i.e. they do the job they need to do. A lot to take in at once I know, but have a look at the Functional Skills tabs as you work through the book and they'll show you what all this means in practice… so that you can use them to help you with your project.

Let's get started!

LOADING VISUAL BASIC

 Click on **Start**, **All Programs** and then follow the menu to **Microsoft Visual Basic 2008 Express Edition**; see Figure Intro.1.

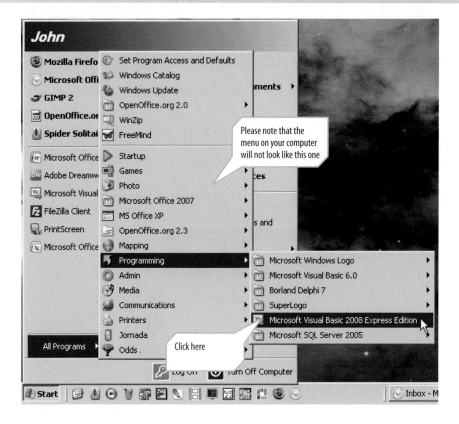

Figure Intro.1

 2 An alternative way to load VB is to double click its icon on the desktop:

VB loads and displays its start page:

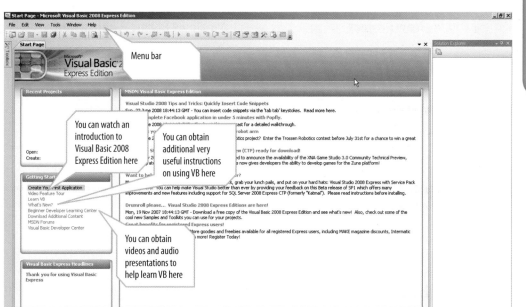

Figure Intro.2

Microsoft has included training with their new version of Visual Basic and Figure Intro.2 shows some of the options for further learning.

THE INTERFACE

An interface is what you see and use on the computer screen.

This could be a view of the flight deck of an aircraft if you are using a computer game with a flight simulator. You would be able to alter some of the aircraft controls by clicking on them and dragging, or use a special joystick to alter the flight of the plane seen on the monitor.

Let's have a look around the VB interface.

1   Click on **File** on the menu bar and select **New Project**:

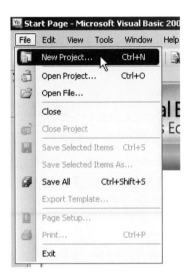

Figure Intro.3

2   In the **New Project** dialogue box, select **Windows Forms Application**:

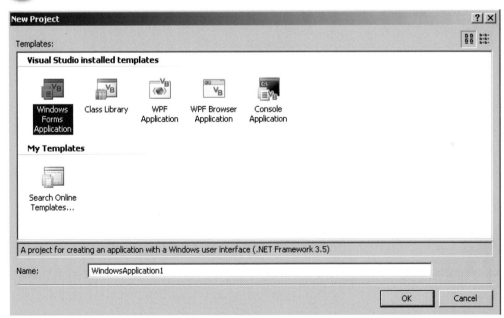

Figure Intro.4

Click **OK**.

It may take a few seconds, but the interface loads showing a form in design view:

TIP

You can also open a new project by clicking the word Project in Create: Project… on the Recent Projects pane of the start page.

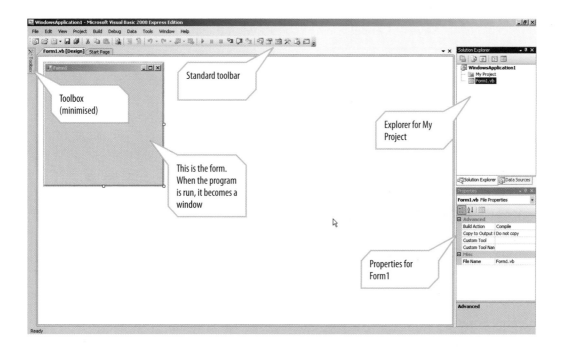

Figure Intro.5

It is useful to have the toolbox permanently maximised. To do this:

 Move the mouse pointer into the **Toolbox** area.

The toolbox immediately expands across the left of the interface.

 Click the **drawing pin icon**, which will 'pin' the toolbox in place:

Figure Intro.6

Objects and controls

The shapes that you see on the monitor screen are called **screen objects**; examples of these would be **icons**, **toolbars**, **mouse pointer**, **window** and so on. The **window** is an important object because we often use it to **contain** other objects; it also has the name **form**, which is used while you are **designing** your program.

There are some screen objects that we can use to make our programs; these are called **controls** because they control how a program works. Examples of controls are the familiar **OK** and **Cancel** buttons that you see when saving your work.

By clicking either **Save** or **Cancel** you can control what the program does next; either it saves your work or just gives up!

Let's have a look at some controls:

 Click on the **Button** control in the toolbox and drag it to the form.

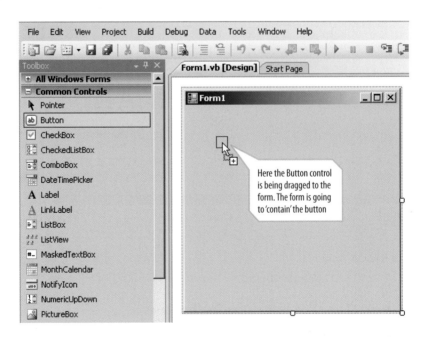

Figure Intro.7

2 Click in about the middle of the form; the button will appear (Figure Intro.8):

 3 Now add a **PictureBox** control to the form (Figure Intro.9):

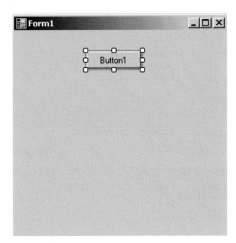

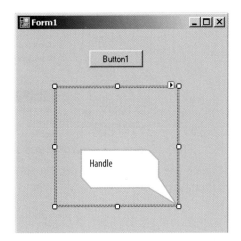

Figure Intro.8 *Figure Intro.9*

 4 Use the **handles** to resize the picture box as necessary.

Properties

A property of a screen object (something visible on the monitor) is a feature such as its colour, what is written on it, its size and its position.

We can change the properties of screen objects in three ways:

> Some properties we can change directly, such as the size of the picture box or position of the button.

> Other properties we can change using the **Properties** pane:

> We can use an **Event Handler** (also called a **Procedure**) to change a property.

This last method is often very useful and we are going to try this out later in this introduction.

We won't bother changing the properties directly because you will already be familiar with changing the size and position of objects on the screen, so first of all let's try changing the properties of the controls on the form using the Properties panel.

 1 Click on the button.

2 Look in the **Properties** panel and notice that it refers to **Button1** (don't worry if for some reason the button is referred to as another name).

SOFTWARE SKILLS
Changing object properties

3 Use the scroll bar on the right of the pane to locate the (Name) property; see Figure Intro.10.

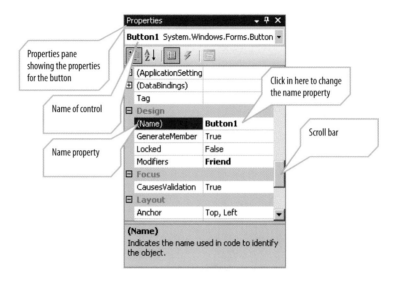

Figure Intro.10

 4 Click in the box, delete '**Button1**' and type in '**cmdShow**'

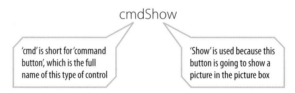

cmdShow

'cmd' is short for 'command button', which is the full name of this type of control

'Show' is used because this button is going to show a picture in the picture box

> **TIP**
>
> *It is good practice to rename controls as you use them because if you leave them with their original names, which do not refer to what they do, you may well have forgotten what they do when you work on the program some time later. Obviously it is best to rename them to something that will remind you of their purpose.*
>
> *A complete list of prefixes can be obtained from www.payne-gallway.co.uk*

Notice that the writing on the button does not change.

 5 Now find the **Text** property for the button and change this to:

Show

 6 Click outside of the Property panel; notice that the button is now labelled Show:

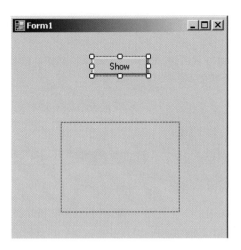

Figure Intro.11

Now click on the **PictureBox** and change its **Name** to:

picShowHide

Use the **Size** property to adjust the size of the picture box to **150 × 150** pixels (see Figure Intro.12).

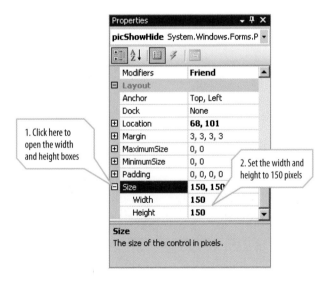

Figure Intro.12

Now click on the form (click on the blue title bar at the top of the form) and change

> its Name to **frmShowHide**

> its Text to **Show and Hide**

> its BackColor to **Red**

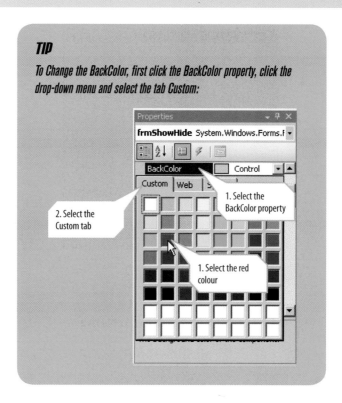

Now the button is coloured red too! Change the button's **BackColor** property to another colour that you prefer; **Control** is used in this example:

Figure Intro.13

Now for the **PictureBox** control.

The idea is this: the PictureBox control is going to contain a picture, *but* it remains hidden until the button is clicked. This means that we will have to set the property for the picture box to be hidden.

 Click on the picture box to highlight it, then find the **BackgroundImage** property:

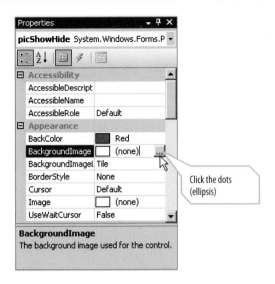

Figure Intro.14

 11 Click next to the word **(none)**. A button with three dots on it appears: click the button.

 12 The **Select Resource** dialogue box appears. This allows us to **import files** (bring them into the project); in this case we want to import a picture for the PictureBox control.

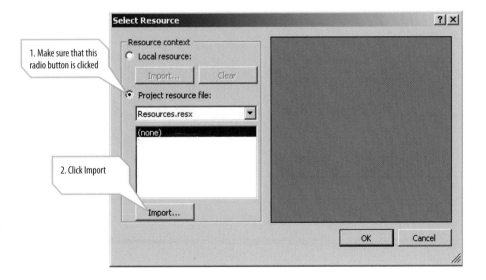

Figure Intro.15

 13 Use the **Open** dialogue box to navigate to the picture file Poppy.jpg

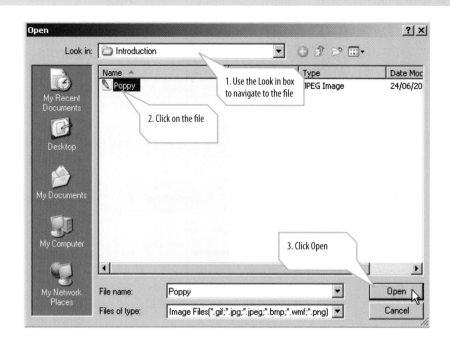

Figure Intro.16

The **Select Resource** dialogue box reappears:

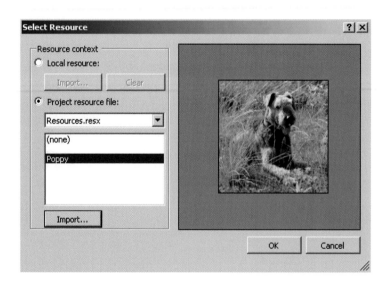

Figure Intro.17

 Check that the name of the file Poppy is highlighted (you click on its name in the dialogue box) and then click **OK**.

Great! Now we have a picture in the PictureBox control:

Figure Intro.18

The last setting is to hide the control … back to the Properties pane!

 15 Find the **Visible** property and use the drop-down box to set it to **False**:

Figure Intro.19

DESIGN TIME AND RUN TIME

So far we have been designing the program and we have not yet tried it out by 'running' it. All of our work so far has been done in **design time**; when we come to actually making the program work on its own, it will run in **run time**.

Debugging

When the program is run, all of its instructions are checked to make sure that the computer can interpret them correctly. This process is called **debugging**. The process automatically starts when you attempt to run the program; see the next section on **Running**.

It is said that the word debugging arose because insects caused faults in early computers, so they literally had to be de-bugged!

Running

Now that we have renamed the controls and set their properties we can try running the program. It won't 'work' yet because there is nothing to connect the button with making the picture box appear, but at least we can check that when the program runs the picture control is hidden.

Look at the standard toolbar:

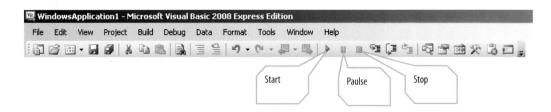

Figure Intro.20

 Click the start icon.

The program runs and displays this screen:

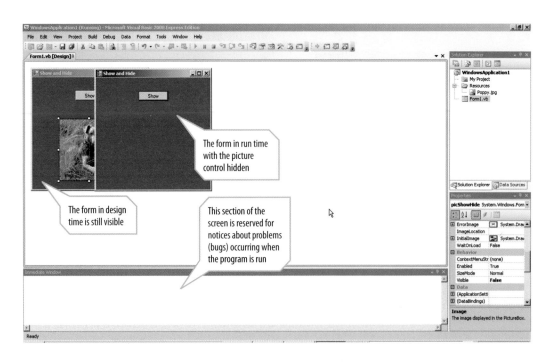

Figure Intro.21

 Click the **Stop** button *twice*.

You are returned to the familiar screen showing the form in design time.

Writing code

RH GSRH RM XLWV?

You will not take long to crack this code! If I wrote the last word as ?XLWV, then even though you know how to convert my code into English, the question mark would mean that the phrase no longer makes sense. When writing code we have to know the code to use (in this case it's just a case of using letters from the opposite end of the alphabet) and we also need to follow rules on how the code is used (in English, we don't put a question mark at the beginning of a word). The rules for writing computer code are called syntax, which would be a good word to remember for when playing 'Hangman'!

We are going to write code to make the picture box appear when the button is pressed.

 Start the code editor by either double clicking on the form or choosing **Code** in the **View** menu on the menu bar.

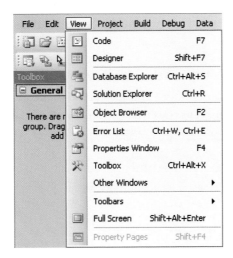

Figure Intro.22

The screen looks a bit intimidating, so let's find our way around:

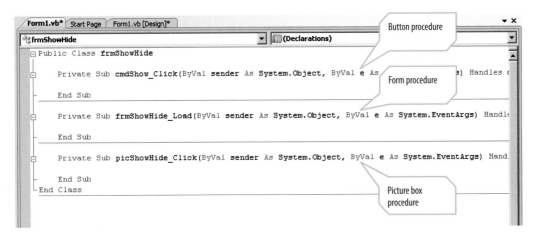

Figure Intro.23

There are three procedures shown in the code view. These are related to the three controls used in the program.

These procedures work as shown in the following table:

Procedure	Type of control	Name of control	Event	Control that is affected	Property to be changed	Method
1	Form	frmShowHide	Load	frmShowHide		
2	Button	cmdShow	Mouse click	picShowHide	Visible=False	Visible=True
3	PictureBox	picShowHide				

Commentary on the table:

Event

This is something which can happen to a control such as a **click** event caused by the user clicking the control using the mouse or a **load** event caused by the program starting.

Method

This is a response to the event: the **click** or **load** event causes the **method** to happen. The method then tells the computer how a change can be made; for example, the click event on the button causes a method to start that causes the visible property of the picture box to change from False (invisible) to True (visible).

The button's **click event** causes a **method** to occur that alters a **property** of the picture box to make it visible. To sum up, our program looks like this:

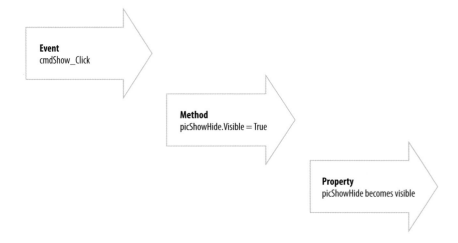

Event
cmdShow_Click

Method
picShowHide.Visible = True

Property
picShowHide becomes visible

 Click underneath **Private Sub cmdShow_Click** and write in the following code:

picShowHide.Visible = True

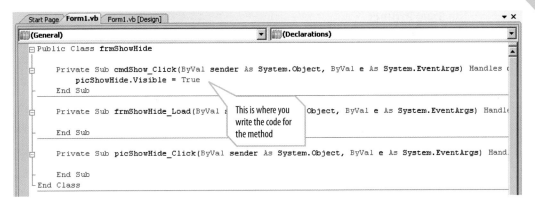

Figure Intro.24

As you write code you will notice that VB tries to help out and offers helpful completion suggestions for what you are writing. You can save time and typing by using the cursor keys to move to the version that you want and accepting this by pressing the **Tab** key.

Try it out!

 Run the program by clicking the Start **Debugging** icon.

By clicking the button, the picture control should become visible together with its picture of Poppy! You can stop the program either by clicking the **X** on the top left of the form ▣ or by clicking the stop button twice. ▣

You can swap back to the view showing the form in design time by using the tabs at the top of the design window:

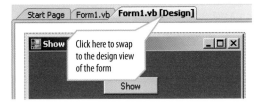

Figure Intro.25

Saving your program

 Click **Save All** in the **File** drop-down menu:

Figure Intro.26

The **Save Project** dialogue box loads:

Figure Intro.27

Type a new file name such as:

ShowHide

into the **Name** box.

Use the **Browse** button.

The **Project Location** dialogue box allows you to move to a location where you want to store your work and to make a new folder:

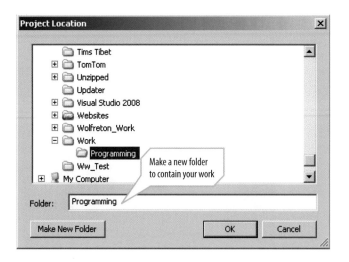

Figure Intro.28

Click **OK**.

Check the details (file name and location) on the **Save Project** dialogue box:

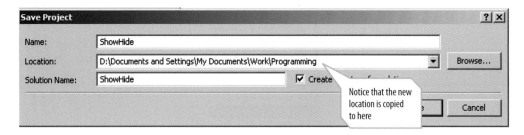

Figure Intro.29

5 Click **Save**.

6 Close VB by clicking the cross icon at the top right of the screen: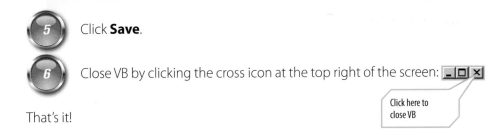

Click here to
close VB

That's it!

GET AHEAD

There are several things you could do to get ready for the next activity in Task 1; here are some suggestions:

❯ Make another button which this time hides the PictureBox control.

❯ Make a button which supplies information for the user. The code for this button is:

The button is
called cmdInfo

```
End Sub

    Private Sub cmdInfo_Click(ByVal sender As System.Object, ByVal e As System.EventArgs) Handles
        MsgBox("Click the Show button to see the picture")
    End Sub
End Class
```

This line is the code
for the new button

Figure Intro.30

❯ Make a button which changes the colour of the form to blue. The code for this button is:

The Name property of
the new button has been
changed to cmdBlue

```
    Private Sub cmdBlue_Click(ByVal sender As System.Object, ByVal e As System.EventArgs) Handles
        Me.BackColor = Color.Blue
    End Sub
End Class
```

This line is the code
for the new button

Figure Intro.31

❯ Make another button which converts the form's BackColor back to its original colour.

Now you've had a chance to play with the software, let's get started on a task.

WHO NEEDS A CALCULATOR?

TASK BRIEF

In Task 1 we are going to make our own calculator that will allow the user to enter two numbers, which it will then add together and display the result. The calculator should only allow numbers to be entered and not letters or punctuation.

This task will allow us to work through some of the important concepts of programming in Visual Basic. Producing a calculator is a useful exercise to do as it means we can check our program is working by adding up the numbers manually to see if we get the same results.

Before we start writing the code for our calculator though, let's try and understand what a line of code is made up of as this will help us to work out what the code will be for our calculator.

TARGET POINT

Have a look at the following statements before you start your task so you know what you are aiming for.

Although you will not make your own decisions on the design of the program in Task 1, you can use what you learn here to help with other work that will be awarded a particular level.

Level 3	Level 4	Level 5	Level 6
You have followed the instructions to produce a form with controls	You have set the properties of the form and controls		
You have followed the instructions and set up a variable	You have incorporated a variable in the instructions of a program that adds two numbers	You have checked that the program works correctly and rectified any errors	
You have written code	You have followed the instructions and written code that assigns a value to a variable	You have shown that you understand how code can be used to change the activity of the computer	
	You have set validation rules for the user input.	You have successfully applied validation to control the user input	You recognise that errors will occur without using some form of validation of the user input

OK, let's get started.

SOFTWARE SKILLS

You will learn how to:

- Design a graphical user interface (GUI)
- Add controls to the GUI
- Set the properties of the controls
- Use events
- Write 'event handler' code, often called procedures, which will control how the program works
- Test your program to make sure that it works correctly
- 'Validate the user input': this means limiting what users can type into the program; for example, not allowing them to try to add together A + B

FUNCTIONAL SKILLS

As you work through this task the Functional Skills tabs will explain to you why the task tackles the brief in the way shown here and explain why you would choose to:

- Recognise and use the features of the interface effectively
- Understand how to use information
- Adapt the program to the needs of the user

CAPABILITY

You are not expected to show capability in this Task because you are following a set of instructions, although if you complete the Get Ahead section you will be working on your own and therefore will be showing capability in making your design more accessible, adapting existing code and using global variables.

VOCABULARY

You should learn these new words and understand what they mean.

- Graphical user interface (GUI)
- Debugging, bug, crash
- Data/information
- Data type (string, char, integer, double)
- Properties, events, event handler/method/procedure
- Input, processing, output
- Variable (local variable, global variable), declaring variables, assigning data to variables
- Memory, memory location
- Compiling
- Validation, validation rules
- Enabled, true, false

RESOURCES

There are no resources for this task

1 Open **Visual Basic 2008 Express Edition** as you did in the Introduction.

2 Once VB has loaded, click **Create: Project** (see Figure 1.1).

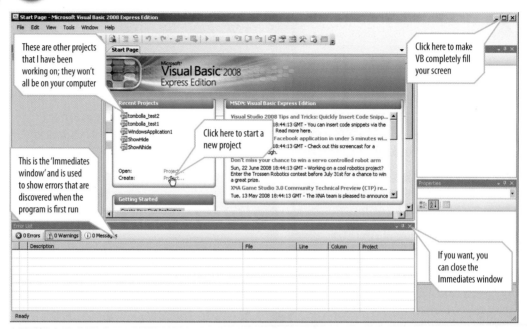

These are other projects that I have been working on; they won't all be on your computer

Click here to make VB completely fill your screen

Click here to start a new project

This is the 'Immediates window' and is used to show errors that are discovered when the program is first run

If you want, you can close the Immediates window

Figure 1.1

3 Make sure that **Windows Forms Application** is highlighted in the **New Project** dialogue box.

4 Type 'MyCalculator' into the Name box and then click **OK**.

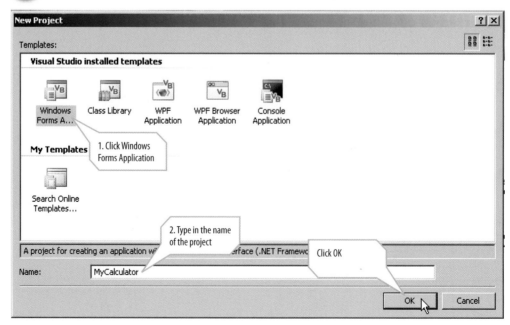

1. Click Windows Forms Application

2. Type in the name of the project

Click OK

Figure 1.2

Once the form loads, you can get on with designing the program.

THE INTERFACE

We are going to make a **graphical user interface** (GUI) for our program. The GUI is the design that appears on the screen when the program loads. You will be familiar with the GUI for MS Word, which allows the user to write on the screen and alter the appearance of the letters by changing the fonts used, and you can probably think of other GUIs that you have come across such as a web browser, a game or the GUI that appears when you log onto the computer. We could, if we wished, not bother and just allow the user to type in two numbers on a blank screen. This wouldn't look as good or be as user friendly, but a very simple program like this with no graphical interface would probably work much faster.

Speed is not going to be an issue for this program; even with a GUI, the computer is going to beat the best maths brains every time!

5   Use the toolbox and draw two text boxes on your form as shown in Figure 1.3.

We shall use these for the two numbers to be added together.

SOFTWARE SKILLS
Using controls to design a GUI

FUNCTIONAL SKILLS
Recognising and using the features of an interface – this includes positioning objects correctly and adjusting object property settings to make your program easier to use

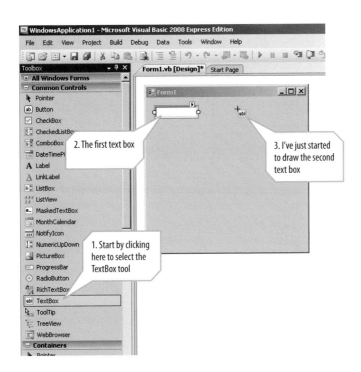

2. The first text box

3. I've just started to draw the second text box

1. Start by clicking here to select the TextBox tool

Figure 1.3

The alignment lines are a useful way to make sure objects line up correctly (Figure 1.4), although there is another method, which we will use in a moment.

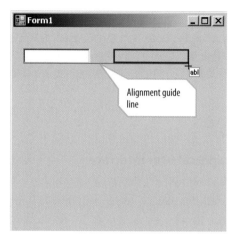

Figure 1.4

 6 Next draw a button on the form (Figure 1.5).

 7 Draw another text box for the answer (Figure 1.6).

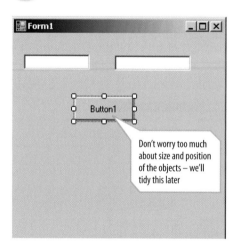

Figure 1.5

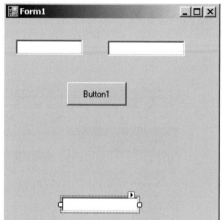

Figure 1.6

PROPERTIES

Now we are going to set the properties for all of the objects. The table only shows the properties that you need to change; all the others stay as they were.

Type of object	Property to change	Setting	Reason
Form	Name	frmCalc	Unique name
	Text	My Calculator	Displayed name
	Size	300, 300	Size is measured in units called pixels
	Locked	True	Stops the user from moving or resizing the form
First text box	Name	txtFirstNumb	
	Location	20, 30	Position on the form in units called pixels, measured from the top left of the form
	Locked	True	
	Size	50, 20	
Second text box	Name	txtSecondNumb	
	Location	220, 30	
	Locked	True	
	Size	50, 20	
Button	Name	cmdCalc	
	Location	110, 100	
	Locked	True	
	Size	80, 30	
	Text	Calculate	
Answer text box	Name	txtAnswer	
	Location	125, 230	
	Locked	True	
	Size	50, 20	

TIP

It is easier to find the properties that you want to change if you list them in alphabetical order first. You do this by clicking the Alphabetical icon in the properties pane:

VB works better if you press the ENTER key on your keyboard after changing each property.

That's the interface completed.

You can try running the program by typing in two numbers in the top two text boxes and using the **Start Debugging** button ▶ to start running the program as we did in the Introduction, but of course nothing will happen because there is no code to link the click of the button to the numbers you type in the input text boxes.

> **TIP**
> *It will pay to read this bit and make sure that you understand all of the ideas that are mentioned.*

Data

Computers don't **understand** anything we store in them; they are just very good at remembering! For example, your name doesn't mean anything to them, but means quite a lot to you, your friends and family!

If you typed your name and password into your school computer, you would be surprised if the computer started a personal conversation with you because you do not expect the computer to understand you as a person with human feelings, but you do expect it to be good at remembering your name and letting you log on. Because computers do not understand, we use the word **data** for anything which is stored on a computer.

Anything with meaning is called **information**. For example, 13 could have meaning for you because it might represent your age or your house number; for others the number will have no meaning and is just data.

Data often becomes information when we can see what it means; for example, 9.8 probably doesn't mean much to you, it's just data! If you jump out of a plane as a sky diver, 9.8 becomes information because this is your rate of acceleration in metres per second per second!

Data types

We have already said that computers do not understand anything. We even have to tell them that

AARDVARK

is data in the form of **letters** and

3.142

Is data in the form a **number** and

is data in the form of an **image**.

Here is a list of **data types** that we will be using in this book:

Name of data type	What it is used for	An example of data for which this data type could be used
String	A word	Aardvark
Char	A single letter	A
Integer	A whole number	123
Double	A fractional number	1.23

Input, processing, output

We often think of what a computer does as having three parts:

> We enter the data – INPUT.

> The computer does something with it – PROCESSING.

> The computer displays the results – OUTPUT.

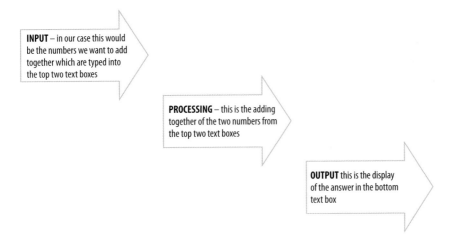

INPUT – in our case this would be the numbers we want to add together which are typed into the top two text boxes

PROCESSING – this is the adding together of the two numbers from the top two text boxes

OUTPUT this is the display of the answer in the bottom text box

Variables

If you were asked to remember the numbers 32 and 112, you might have difficulty remembering them in a week's time. If I told you that in the temperature scale Farenheit, 32 is the freezing point of water and 112 is normally taken as water's boiling point, then there is more of a chance you will remember the information. What you have done is associate the number with the behaviour of water. We use this all the time to help remember facts – for example, we can recall the colours and their order in the rainbow using the phrase 'Richard Of York Gave Battle In Vain', where the R of Richard means Red, etc.

We give a label to any information we want the computer to remember. When we want the computer to find the information, we remind them of the label and the computer retrieves the data from its memory.

These labels are called variables and we are going to use them in our program to store numbers.

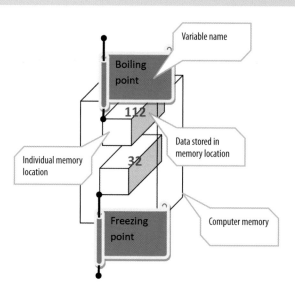

Figure 1.7

To sum up:

❯ The computer's memory is a number of boxes into which we can put **data** that we want the computer to store.

❯ We tell the computer to remember the data by a name attached to it.

❯ This name is called a **variable** and can be more or less any word, but is best if the variable name reminds us humans of the data that is being stored.

❯ It wouldn't be wise to name the data to be stored in our calculator program after your favourite pet or sports team because, although the computer wouldn't mind, you would not remember what was being stored from just looking at the name.

Types of variable

There are two types of variable which you will come across soon:

❯ **Global variables**. These are 'known about' by all of the program. For example, each of your friends knows your name.

❯ **Local variables**. These are 'known about' by only a single part of the program where it is being used, for example a button. The rest of the program just ignores the variable. For example, only your doctor knows your blood group.

Declaring variables

The word **As** is used to warn the computer that you are about to tell it what type of data is going to be stored in a variable. This process is called **declaring a variable**. Here is an example:

Dim AnimalName As String

This is a special ('reserved') word which warns the computer that you are telling it the name of a variable

This is the name of the variable

This is a special ('reserved') word which warns the computer that you are about to tell it the type of data that will be stored in the computer using this variable

This is a word used to tell the computer that the data to be stored will be letters – see table on page 29

This line means:

**'Hello computer, set up a place in your memory for storing some letters
and call this place AnimalName'**

Or, if you prefer to think of this as a picture:

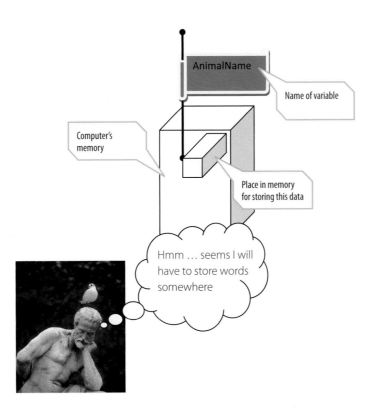

AnimalName

Name of variable

Computer's
memory

Place in memory
for storing this data

Hmm … seems I will
have to store words
somewhere

Assigning data to variables

SOFTWARE SKILLS
Assigning data to a variable

Once we have declared the variables, we have 'post boxes' in the computer's memory. The
next stage is to put something in them – this is called assigning data to the variables.

It's quite easy to do; have a look at this example:

AnimalName = Aardvark

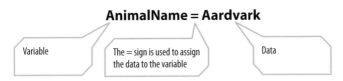

Variable

The = sign is used to assign
the data to the variable

Data

Once the computer reads this section of code it will place the word Aardvark in a place in
its memory which it knows is called AnimalName.

Later on you may wish to replace Aardvark with Platypus. Simple – write this code:

AnimalName = Platypus

and the job's done! Unlike us, the computer has immediately forgotten about Aardvark
and now knows only Platypus. Can you think why this has happened?

Yes, the computer has replaced the word Aardvark with Platypus in the **same** memory location. Computers can remember many pieces of data, but a memory location can only remember one piece of data at a time.

You can also assign data that a user types into the computer to a variable; for example, in our program, where the user types a number into one of the text boxes.

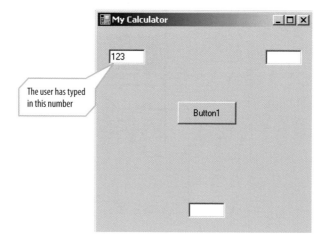

Figure 1.8

Typing the number into the text box alters its **Text** property: it was blank, now it contains a number.

The next line of code **assigns the data in the text box** to the **variable** FirstNumb:

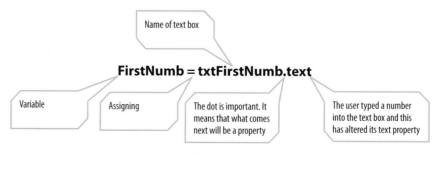

> **TIP**
>
> *Don't worry if this seems a bit difficult to grasp. There are a lot of ideas here and they will only fall into place once you can see how the code is written and is used by the computer.*
>
> *Use this section as a reference; you can always come back to this later.*

Writing code

This is what controls the processing. These are the instructions to tell the computer what to do.

We need to tell it to do something with the numbers in the text boxes when a user clicks the button.

 Double click the button to open the code editor:

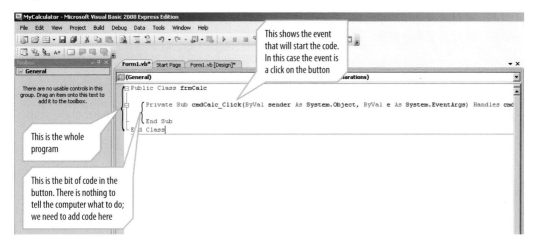

Figure 1.9

First of all we need to set up the variables. We will need the following variables in our program:

Type of variable	Name of variable	Where we are going to use the variable	Purpose of the variable
Local	FirstNumb	The button named cmdCalc	As a label for the number the user types into the text box named txtFirstNumb
Local	SecondNumb	The button named cmdCalc	As a label for the number the user types into the text box named txtSecondNumb
Local	AnsNumb	The button named cmdCalc	As a label for the answer the computer puts into the text box named txtAnswer

 Click where indicated on Figure 1.10.

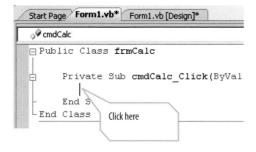

Figure 1.10

Now to declare the variables:

10 Type in the variables.

Notice that, as you type, VB tries to be helpful:

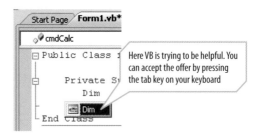

Figure 1.11

11 Figure 1.12 shows you what to type. Remember: check you are entering the variables into the event handler for the button!

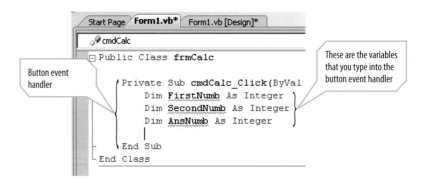

Figure 1.12

We need to add code to the button event handler to make the button click event add together the numbers in the two top text boxes.

This is the code and what it does: We need to get the computer to:

❯ Get the number from the txtFirstNumb text box and store it in the variable called FirstNumb.

❯ Get the number from the txtSecondNumb text box and store it in the variable called SecondNumb.

❯ Add the numbers together.

❯ Store the result in the variable called AnsNumb.

❯ Write this variable in the txtAnswer text box.

We can get the computer to do this by writing the following code:

Code to be typed into the button click event handler	What the code means
FirstNumb = txtFirstNumb.text	The number that the user enters in the first text box (the 'text') is assigned to the variable FirstNumb
SecondNumb = txtSecondNumb.text	The number that the user enters in the second text box (the 'text') is assigned to the variable SecondNumb
AnsNumb = FirstNumb + SecondNumb	The data in the variables FirstNumb and SecondNumb are added together and this is then assigned to the variable AnsNumb
txtAnswer.text = AnsNumb	The data in AnsNumb is displayed in the text box txtAnswer

 12 Now enter this code into the cmdCalc click event.

You will notice that VB is helpful as usual and you do not need to type very much – just accept the code elements using the tab key.

Check the code elements offered by VB – it can't read your mind!

Your code should look like this (extra blank lines don't matter):

```
Start Page  Form1.vb  Form1.vb [Design]
cmdCalc                                      Click
Public Class frmCalc

    Private Sub cmdCalc_Click(ByVal sender As System.Object, ByVal e As System.EventArgs) Handles cmd
        Dim FirstNumb As Integer
        Dim SecondNumb As Integer
        Dim AnsNumb As Integer

        FirstNumb = txtFirstNumb.Text
        SecondNumb = txtSecondNumb.Text
        AnsNumb = FirstNumb + SecondNumb
        txtAnswer.Text = AnsNumb

    End Sub
End Class
```

Figure 1.13

If you make a mistake, very often VB will spot it and show you where the problem is by underlining some of the code with a wiggly line like this:

```
Start Page  Form1.vb*  Form1.vb [Design]*
(General)                                    (Declarations)
Public Class frmCalc

    Private Sub cmdCalc_Click(ByVal sender As System.Object, ByVal e As System.EventArgs) Handles cmd
        Dim FirstNumb As Integer
        Dim SecondNumb                You can see the
        Dim AnsNumb As               mistake here. Note
                                     the blue wiggly line
        FirstNumb = txt
        SecondNumb =
        AnsNumb = F  stNumb + SecondNumb
        txtAnswer.Te = AnsNumb

    End Sub
End Class
```

Figure 1.14

It's time to test the program!

 Click the **Start Debugging** button ▷ on the standard toolbar.

This starts VB turning your program code that you wrote in English into a language that the computer understands. This process is called **compiling**.

 Once the VB has compiled your program the screen will look something like that shown in Figure 1.15.

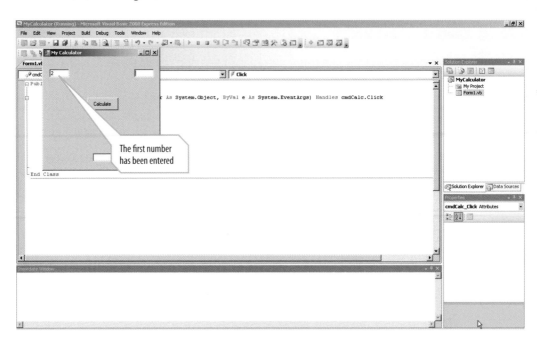

Figure 1.15

 Type numbers 2 and 3 into the top two text boxes and click the **Calculate** button.

Figure 1.16

16 Delete the numbers and try some others.

Now try the numbers 2.4 and 3.4

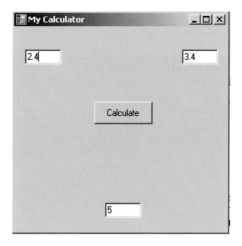

Figure 1.17

You would expect the answer text box to show 5.8 but it doesn't. It shows 5! Any ideas why this should have happened?

Remember that the variables were set up to contain **whole** numbers (the data type is **Integer**). This means that fractions cannot be used unless we change the data type for the variables to **Double**, which instructs the computer to accept fractional numbers, 1.234 for example.

17 Click on the cross on the top right of the form to stop the program running and return to the design time view:

Make sure it is this X that you click!

Figure 1.18

18 Change the data type for all three variables to **Double**:

```
Start Page  Form1.vb  Form1.vb [Design]

(General)                                                    (Declarations)

Public Class frmCalc

    Private Sub cmdCalc_Click(ByVal sender As System.Object, ByVal e As System.EventArgs) Handles cmd
        Dim FirstNumb As Double
        Dim SecondNumb As Double
        Dim AnsNumb As Double

        FirstNumb = txtFirstNumb.Text
        SecondNumb = txtSecondNumb.Te       Notice the change
        AnsNumb = FirstNumb + SecondNum      of data type
        txtAnswer.Text = AnsNumb

    End Sub
End Class
```

Figure 1.19

Now test the program:

 Click the **Start Debugging** button.

 Enter the values 2.4 and 3.4 in the top two text boxes and click **Calculate**.

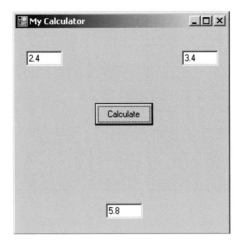

Figure 1.20

Well, that seems to have cured the problem.

Oh no! What if someone tries to type in **two** instead of **2**? There is only one way to find out: try it!

And the result is:

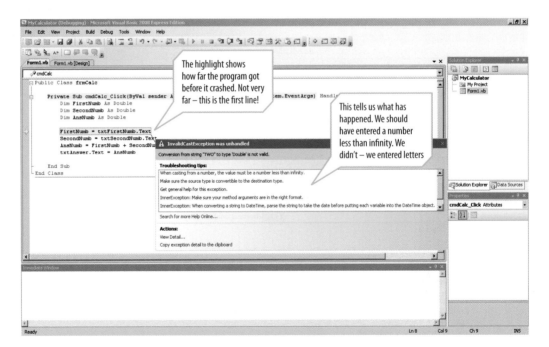

Figure 1.21

Oops! This is called a program crash.

21 Click the **Stop Debugging** button:

Return to the designer view so that you can change the properties of the screen objects.

 22 Click the **View Designer** button in the **Solution Explorer** pane: 🔲

We need to prevent the user from entering inappropriate data such as letters which will cause program crashes; we'll do that next.

Setting up validation

Here's a quick review of the situation so far.

You have a calculator that works even for fractional numbers, but users can crash the program by entering inappropriate data types such as letters. You are going to stop this from happening by preventing the entry of data other than numbers into the input text boxes. This important aspect of programming is called **data validation**.

Masked text boxes

You will need to replace the user input text boxes (the ones at the top of the screen) with **masked text boxes**. These have extra properties which we can use to control the user input and stop letters from being typed into the program.

 23 Delete the top two text boxes by clicking on them and pressing delete.

 24 Replace the text boxes with **masked text boxes**:

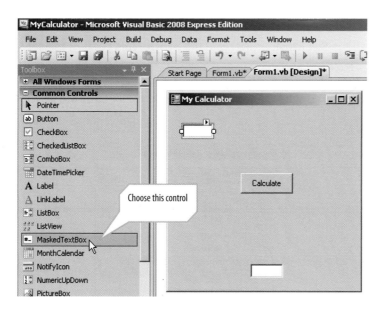

Figure 1.22

 25 Repeat this for the second masked text box.

 26 Now look back to page 27 and use the table to set the properties for the new text box to the same values as you used for the originals.

SOFTWARE SKILLS
Using validation to control user input

27 Run the program by clicking the **Start Debugging** button.

 28 Enter numbers in the new masked text boxes. Choose numbers that you can easily add in your head.

 29 Click the **Calculate** button.

 30 Does the program work – is the answer correct?

TIP

If the program does not work, it is almost certain that the problem lies in the properties of the masked text boxes: check these carefully for mistakes in copying form the table, particularly the Name property.

Validating data input

Now that you have setup the masked text boxes for the user data input, you can move on to making them accept numbers and reject any other type of input.

 31 Stop the program running by clicking the **X** in the top right of the form or by clicking the **Stop Debugging** button twice.

 32 Make sure that you can see the **screen objects** (the controls for the form, text boxes and command button). If you can't then click the **View Design** button [icon] in the **Solution Explorer** pane or use the menus to select **View > Designer**.

To set the validation for the input text boxes you need to change a property called **Set Mask**. You can find this property either in the normal way by clicking the masked text box and then finding the **Set Mask** property in the **Properties** pane of the screen, or there is a quick shortcut, which we are going to use now:

 33 Right click on the first **masked text box** and select **Set Mask** from the shortcut menu.

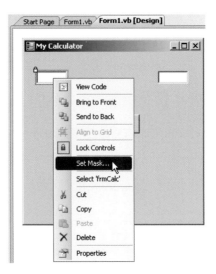

Figure 1.23

The **Input Mask** dialogue box loads:

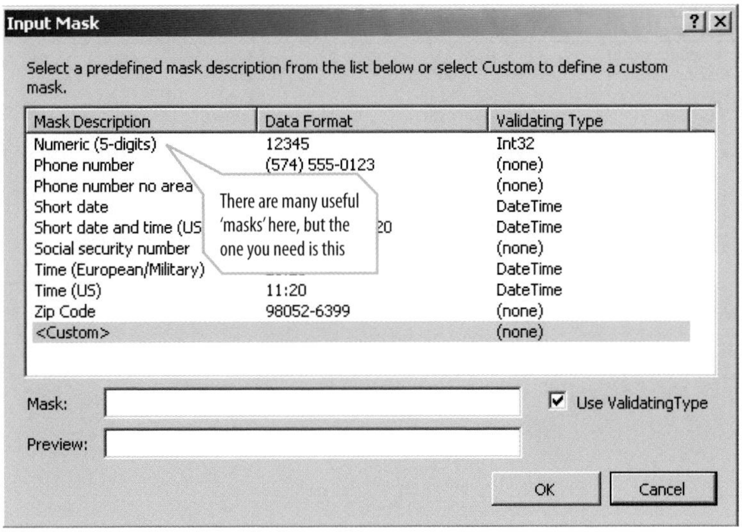

Figure 1.24

34 Click the first option – **Numeric (5-digits)**. Notice the code used for the mask (00000).

35 Click **OK**.

Test plan

Now run the program again to check its function by using this test plan:

> Users are able to enter up to 5 digits, for example 12345.

> Users are not able to enter text.

> The program calculates accurately.

> The user is able to use fractional numbers such as 1234.5.

You will notice that the mask has prevented users from using the point '**.**' in fractional numbers and we will tackle this next.

36 Stop the program from running and return to the design view.

37 Right click on the first text box and select **Set Mask** as you did previously.

Now change the mask:

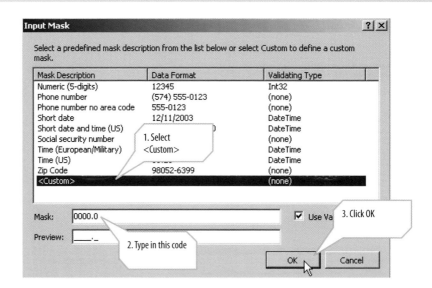

Figure 1.25

 38 Run the program again to check all of the above tests.

If your program runs successfully, then apply the changes to the second text box and run through the test plan again to check that the program still functions correctly.

Tab index

It is useful to find that the cursor is already in the first text box when the program loads and that you can move to the next control using the **Tab** key on the keyboard.

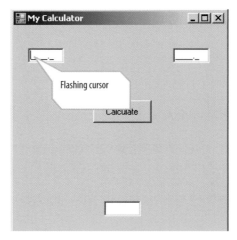

Figure 1.26

To do this you need to stop the program if it is still running and return to design view.

 39 Click on the top-left text box and find **TabIndex** in the **Properties** pane:

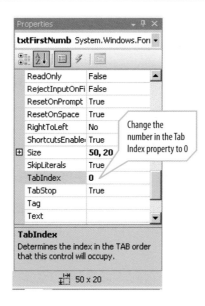

Figure 1.27

40 Change the number in the listing to 0

41 Click on the top-right text box and change its **TabIndex** property to 1.

42 Click on the Calculate button and change its **TabIndex** property to 2.

Controlling access to the answer text box

You don't need users to access the answer text box, so change its **Enabled** property to **False**.

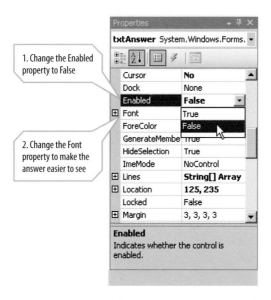

Figure 1.28

43 The current font doesn't show up too well in the non-enabled text box which has a grey background, so change the font property to **Bold**, size **12**.

 44 You will need to adjust the **Size** to **55, 26** and **TextAlign** to **Center**.

 45 Check the running of the program again using the test plan.

SUPPLYING A CLEAR BUTTON

At the moment the user has to clear the input text boxes before another number can be entered. It would be more convenient for the user to click a button to clear both boxes – this is how to set this up:

 46 Return to design view and draw another button on the form:

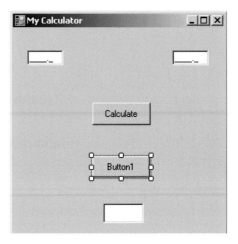

Figure 1.29

 47 Change the properties of this new button as shown in the following table:

Type of object	Property to change	Setting	Reason
Button	Name	cmdClear	Unique name
	Location	110, 150	
	Locked	True	
	Size	80,30	
	Text	Clear	Text to appear on the button
	TabIndex	5	Last tab, which corresponds to the last action by the user

 48 Run the program again to check that the button appears correctly.

Stop the program and return to design view.

We need to look at the new code that is to be written into cmdClear:

Code to be typed into the button click event handler	What the code means
txtFirstNumb.Text = ("")	The text property of the first text box is changed so that it is empty; there is nothing between the speech marks
txtSecondNumb.Text = ("")	The text property of the second text box is changed so that it is empty; there is nothing between the speech marks
txtAnswer.Text = ("")	The text property of the answer text box is changed so that it is empty; there is nothing between the speech marks

 Swap to code view by double clicking **cmdClear**.

 Type in the new code:

SOFTWARE SKILLS
Writing code to clear controls

```
Private Sub Button1_Click(ByVal sender As System.Object, ByVal

        txtFirstNumb.Text = ("")
        txtSecondNumb.Text = ("")
        txtAnswer.Text = ("")

    End Sub
End Class
```

Figure 1.30

 Now run the program and carry out the test plan as before to check that the program is reliable. The test plan is not really complete now that new functions have been added, so now would be a good idea to devise your own, more complete plan.

 Save your work by clicking on **File** and selecting **Save All** from the drop-down menu:

That's it!

GET AHEAD

There is quite a lot you could do to the program to make it more useful, or to just make it look better. As you are working on your own, you will be showing 'capability'. Here are a few ideas to get you going:

 Change the colour of the form and controls by changing their properties.

2 Change the size of the fonts so that the calculator is suitable for the young or partially sighted.

3 Add another button. Copy and adapt the existing code so that the calculator can subtract. You could extend this idea so that the calculator can multiply and divide too! The code will be just the same as you used for the addition button, except that you will need to:

> Declare your variables globally (see later instructions for this). The reason for this is that *each* button event handler will need to know about the variables so that they all have access to the data that has been stored in the variables. If you don't do this and rely on local variables, the numbers typed into the input text boxes by the user will only be accessible by *one* of the buttons.

> Set the properties for the buttons. This should be easy, though, now that you have had a lot of experience in setting properties.

> Use * for multiply (hold down the shift key then press the 8 key on your keyboard).

> Use / for divide (just next to the full stop on your keyboard).

Remember, this program is a free download from Microsoft so if you want to use a copy at home and amaze your friends with your programming skills, then go to:

http://www.microsoft.com/express/

Global variables

This screen shot shows the variables being moved from **local** to **global**:

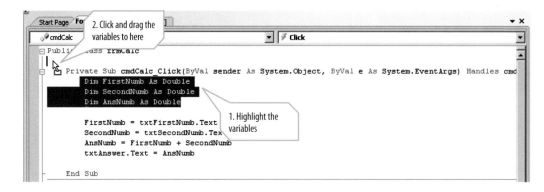

Figure 1.31

CHECKPOINT

Check that you know how to:

> Use controls to design a GUI

> Declare a variable

> Assign data to a variable

> Write code to change the properties of a control

> Use validation methods to control the user input

> Test the program and put right errors

ASSESSMENT POINT

Now let's assess the work. Look back at the table at the beginning of this section (**Target point**) and decide on which of the statements you can answer 'Yes' to.

Did you do as well as you expected? Could you improve your work? Use Word to write a comment to show what you could do to improve your work and remember this when starting your next ICT project.

TASK BRIEF

In this task you will build a 'fruit machine'.

These are often used by charities to raise money for good causes. A player pays a small sum for their turn and when the machine runs it displays a number of pictures, often of fruit, hence the name fruit machine. If the pictures are of all of the same fruit, then a prize is awarded.

In our fruit machine, there will be only two pictures; a picture of a cat and a picture of a dog. The computer will select either picture on a random basis and if, after three selections, the player has either three dog pictures or three cat pictures, they will have won.

This would be a winning line-up:

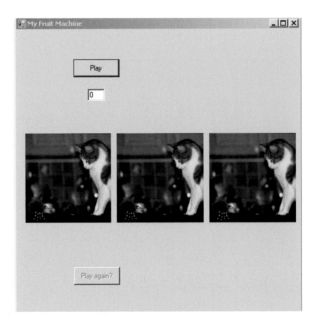

Figure 2.1

So would three dogs!

SOFTWARE SKILLS

You will learn how to:

➤ Use and understand variables including arrays

➤ Assign data to variables including arrays

➤ Use and understand the use of local and global variables

➤ Store images in the Resources folder

➤ Use a random number generating function

➤ Use an element index to assign data to an array

➤ Use a selection construct

➤ Use a counting system

➤ Duplicate code

➤ Edit code

FUNCTIONAL SKILLS

As you work through this task the Functional Skills tabs will explain to you why the task tackles the brief in the way shown here and explain why you would choose to:

➤ Use navigation tools

➤ Understand how to set properties of objects and controls

➤ Customise your project

CAPABILITY

You are not expected to show capability in this Task because you are following a set of instructions, although if you complete the Get Ahead section you will be working on your own and therefore will be showing capability in fine-tuning your form design and altering the game so that it can be played repeatedly without the need to reload it.

VOCABULARY

You should learn these new words and understand what they mean.

➤ Array

➤ Element

➤ Index

➤ Selection construct

➤ Random number

➤ If… Then… End If

 TARGET POINT

Turn the page to see your Target Points for this task.

	Level 3	Level 4	Level 5	Level 6
	You have followed the instructions to declare a local variable	You have followed instructions to declare a global variable	You show that you understand the use of local and global variables	
		You have declared an array	You have successfully assigned data to an element of an array	You have shown that you understand the use of arrays in storing related information and simplifying a computer program
				You have used the index of an element in an array to assign an image to a picture box
	You have followed the instructions to write a selection construct using If… Then… End If		You have successfully incorporated a selection construct to control placing of a picture in a picture box	You have shown that you understand how the If… Then… End If selection construct controls the program
	You have followed the instructions to write a random number generating routine		You have successfully incorporated a random function in the code of the program	You have shown that you understand the use of a random function in the program

OK, let's get started.

 Open **Visual Basic 2008 Express Edition** as you did in the Introduction and Task 1.

 Once VB has loaded, click **Create: Project** (see Figure 2.2)

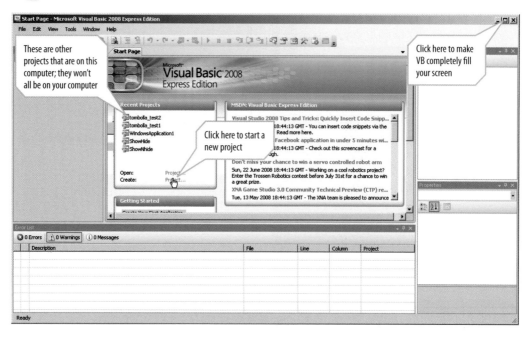

Figure 2.2

In the **New Project** dialogue box, click on **Windows Forms Application** and then rename the application:

FruitMachine

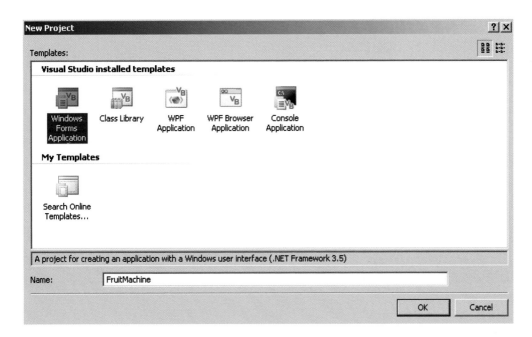

Figure 2.3

 Click **OK**.

TIP

If you want to reload your project, you may find that VB does not automatically load the form. If this happens, click the form in the solution explorer:

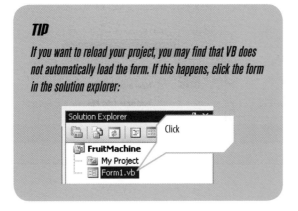

Once the form has loaded you can start to design the GUI, but first of all let's make sure that the resources are ready to be used.

 Double click **My Project**

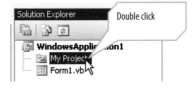

Figure 2.4

The **project designer** window opens:

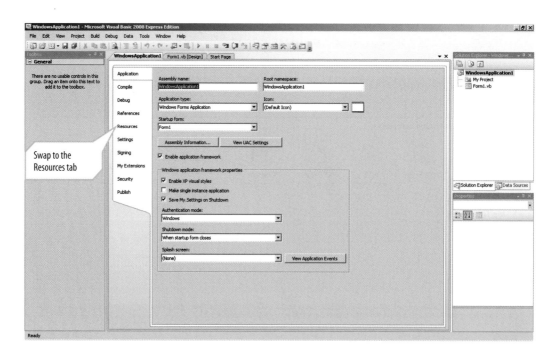

Figure 2.5

 Click on the **Resources** tab:

Figure 2.6

 Click the down triangle to open the **Add Resource** menu and select (click) **Add Existing File**.

Use the **Add existing file to resources** dialogue box to navigate to where the file

Poppy.jpg

is found on your computer system. The location of the file will be different to that shown here.

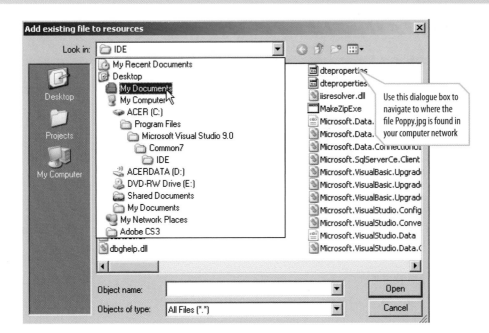

FUNCTIONAL SKILLS

Finding your way around the stored files – it is important to know how to use the navigation tools in your operating system so that you can access your stored files easily

Figure 2.7

9 When you find the file, click on its file name and then click **Open**.

TIP

You can select both Poppy.jpg and Murphy.jpg by clicking one file name and then holding down the Ctrl key on your keyboard while clicking the other.

Once they are both selected, click Open.

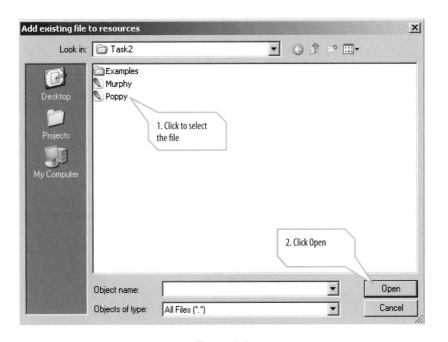

Figure 2.8

You will see both files added to a new folder called Resources in the **Solution Explorer** pane:

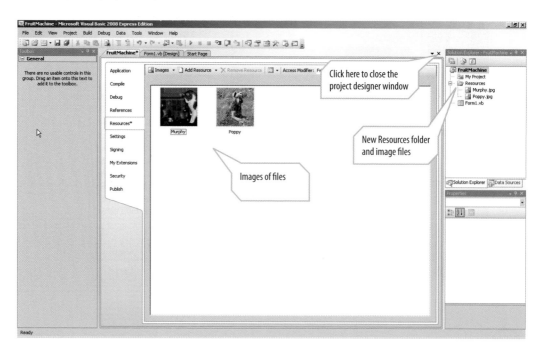

Figure 2.9

10 Close the project designer (see Figure 2.9).

VB will prompt you to save changes to the Resources folder files.

11 Click **Yes**.

Now that we have the resources in place we can start designing the interface.

DESIGNING THE GRAPHICAL USER INTERFACE

Stage 1: adding the controls

Have a look at Figure 2.10, which gives an idea of what you are aiming for.

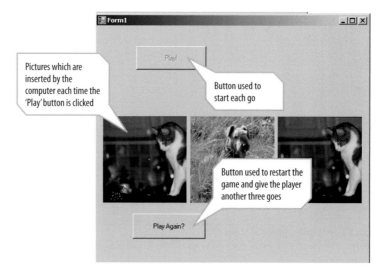

Figure 2.10

12 Make sure that the **Common Controls** tab of the toolbox is open and then drag the following controls onto the form. Do not worry about their size or position at this stage:

> ❱ Two buttons
> ❱ Three picture boxes
> ❱ One text box

Stage 2: setting the properties

Click on the object/control whose properties you want to change and then set them as in this table:

Type of object	Property to change	Setting	Reason
Form	Name	frmFruit	Unique name for the form
	Text	My Fruit Machine	Displayed name
	Size	500,500	Size is measured in units called pixels
	Locked	True	Stops the user from moving or resizing the form
First button	Name	cmdPlay	Unique name for the button
	Text	Play	Displayed text to inform the user of the use of the button
	Enabled	True	This will mean that the user is able to click the button. You will probably find that the button already has this setting
	Location	100, 50	Position on the form in units called pixels, measured from the top left of the form
	Locked	True	
	Size	80, 30	
Second button	Name	cmdAgain	Unique name for the button
	Text	Play again?	Displayed text inviting the user to try again
	Enabled	False	This will mean that the user cannot click the button at the start of the game
	Location	100, 400	
	Locked	True	
	Size	50,20	
First picture box	Name	picFirst	Unique name for the first picture box
	Enabled	True	
	Location	15, 175	
	Locked	True	
	Size	150, 150	
Second picture box	Name	picSecond	Unique name for the second picture box
	Enabled	True	
	Location	175, 175	
	Locked	True	
	Size	150, 150	

Type of object	Property to change	Setting	Reason
Third picture box	Name	picThird	Unique name for the third picture box
	Enabled	True	
	Location	325, 175	
	Locked	True	
	Size	150, 150	
Text box	Name	txtRanNum	Unique name for the text box
	Enabled	True	
	Location	125,100	
	Locked	True	
	Size	30,20	

Check through the properties to make sure you haven't missed anything, then try running the program as you did in Task 1 by clicking the **Start Debugging** button on the standard toolbar:

The picture boxes will not be visible when the program is run and cmdAgain will be greyed out and not useable:

TIP
If you need to save your work click File and then Save All:

Figure 2.11

WRITING THE CODE

The rules of the game

They are quite simple.

➤ Every user has three goes and clicks the **Play** button each time they have a go.

➤ Clicking the Play button causes the computer to randomly select either the number 1 or the number 0.

➤ In the first go, if the computer selects 1, the picture of a dog goes into the **first** picture box. If the computer selects 0, then the picture of the cat goes into the first picture box. This will be the end of the first go.

➤ For the second go, the computer does exactly the same, *except* the picture of the dog or cat goes into the **second** picture box.

➤ For the third go, the computer does exactly the same, *except* the picture of the dog or cat goes into the **third** picture box.

➤ If all three pictures are the same, they have won. If the pictures are different then they lose.

Step 1: choosing the variables

We will need to use **global** variables that will be used by several parts of the program and **local** variables that will only be used by one part of the program.

The variable PetNumb has to store **two** pictures, the dog and the cat. This is impossible for an ordinary variable, so we shall use an **Array** that has two different parts called **elements**, one element for each picture.

Another array has to be used for storing the random number because there are three random numbers, one from each go.

The following table summarises the variables we will use:

Type of variable	Name of variable	Where we are going to use the variable	Purpose of the variable	Data type
Local This is an array. We use an array here so that we can make two versions of the variable and use one for each picture	PetNumber(0)	The button called cmdPlay	Stores the picture of the cat	Image
Local	PetNumber(1)	The button called cmdPlay	Stores the picture of the dog	Image
Global	NumberGoes	Throughout the program	Counts the number of goes	Integer

Type of variable	Name of variable	Where we are going to use the variable	Purpose of the variable	Data type
Global This is an array. We use an array here so that we can make two versions of the variable and use one for each picture	PickedNumber(0)	Throughout the program	Stores the random number (0 or 1) for the first go	Integer
Global	PickedNumber(1)	Throughout the program	Stores the random number (0 or 1) for the second go	Integer
Global	PickedNumber(2)	Throughout the program	Stores the random number (0 or 1) for the third go	Integer
Global	i	Throughout the program	Stores the number of times that parts of the program are repeated (see the loop example on pages 84–85)	Integer

Step 2: declaring the variables

Let's put the variables into the program now.

You will need to swap to the code view.

 Either double click on the form *or* click the **View Code** button ▣ in the **Solution Explorer** pane.

There are two new ideas in this task, global variables and arrays. We'll deal with these new ideas first:

Global variables

We are going to declare the global variables first. These are variables that can be used by all parts of the program and it is important to declare them beneath '**Public Class frmFruit**' as can be seen in Figure 2.12; otherwise they will not act as global variables.

You write the global variables under the line that separates off the public class frmFruit, but as soon as you press the Enter key, the line moves down beneath the new variable.

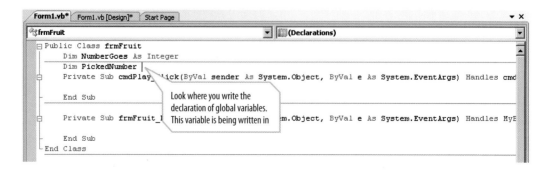

Figure 2.12

Arrays

You declare an array like this:

the name of the array followed by the number of elements (parts) you want in the array, starting with 0 as the first part.

For example:

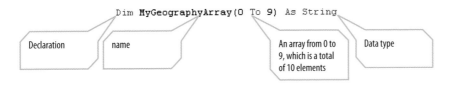

Figure 2.13

So you could use the array to store ten items of data; in the example here an array is being used to store the names of cities. Arrays are very useful in programs because if we want to refer to the data we can just give a reference to the number in the '**Index**' of the element in the array. For example, if we reference index 7, we will find the element containing the data 'Berlin'.

Label	Element index	Data in the element
MyGeographyArray	0	London
MyGeographyArray	1	Paris
MyGeographyArray	2	New York
MyGeographyArray	3	Beijing
MyGeographyArray	4	Tokyo
MyGeographyArray	5	Delhi
MyGeographyArray	6	Rome
MyGeographyArray	7	Berlin
MyGeographyArray	8	Madrid
MyGeographyArray	9	Prague

Entering the variables

 14 Enter all of the variables so that they are written as shown in Figure 2.13. You can see the completed version in Figure 2.14.

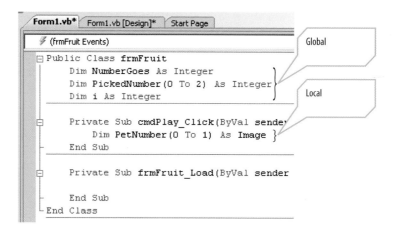

Figure 2.14

Notice that you have entered declarations for two arrays (PickedNumber and PetNumber).

SOFTWARE SKILLS

Writing code to generate a random number

Step 3: writing code that generates the random numbers

The next stage is to make the computer randomly produce either a 1 or a 0. There are two pieces of code we need to write.

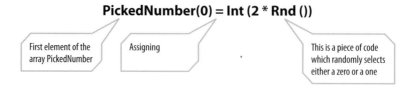

The first line just tells the computer to get ready to select a number randomly. This is set by the word:

Randomize

The second piece of code tells the computer that the random number must be either a 1 or a 0 and then assigns the random number to the array element PickedNumber(0).

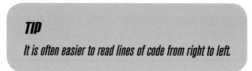

PickedNumber(0) = Int (2 * Rnd ())

First element of the array PickedNumber	Assigning	This is a piece of code which randomly selects either a zero or a one

You are not expected to fully understand this code, just concentrate on how it is written in the above diagram and remember it is a good idea to read from right to left.

Now that we have an idea of how the piece of code works, we can start to write code into the cmdPlay event handler.

 15   Click after the declaration of the PetNumber array in the cmdPlay event handler:

```
┌─ Public Class frmFruit
│      Dim NumberGoes As Integer
│      Dim PickedNumber(0 To 2) As Integer
│      Dim i As Integer
│
├─     Private Sub cmdPlay_Click(ByVal sender
│          Dim PetNumber(0 To 1) As Image
├─     End Sub
│
├─     Private Sub frmFruit_Load(ByVal sender
│
├─     End Sub
└─ End Class
```

Click here

Figure 2.15

 16 Press the **Enter** key to move down to the next line then enter the code in Figure 2.16, pressing the Enter key at the end of each line of code. Remember that you can accept the code offered by VB by pressing the **Tab** key.

```
Start Page  Form1.vb  Form1.vb [Design]

cmdPlay                                                   ▼   ⚡ Click

┌─ Public Class frmFruit
│      Dim NumberGoes As Integer
│      Dim PickedNumber(0 To 2) As Integer
│      Dim i As Integer
│
├─     Private Sub cmdPlay_Click(ByVal sender As System.Object, ByVა
│          Dim PetNumber(0 To 1) As Image
│          Randomize()
│          PickedNumber(0) = Int(2 * Rnd())
│          TxtRanNum.Text = PickedNumber(0)
├─     End Sub                              New code
│
├─     Private Sub frmFruit_Load(ByVal sender As          t, ByVა
│
├─     End Sub
└─ End Class
```

Figure 2.16

The last line of code changes the **Text** property of the text box so that it displays the random number selected by the computer.

TxtRanNum.Text = PickedNumber (0)

This is the name of the text box

This is the property we are going to change

This contains the randomly selected number

Now try it out!

It is best to run your code periodically just to check that it works and to avoid the problem of trying to find errors in large amounts of code.

 17 Click the **Start Debugging** icon on the standard toolbar: ▶

The program should run and appear similar to Figure 2.17:

Figure 2.17

Click the Play button and check that *both* 1 and 0 occur in the text box.

You will probably have to click Play several times.

Check that *both* 1 and 0 can display in the text box. Because 1 and 0 are selected randomly don't expect a 0 to be followed by a 1, you may have to click several times before the program will have displayed each of them in the text box.

If the program doesn't work correctly, stop it running by clicking the **X** at the top right of the form (see Figure 2.17) and check through the code carefully. Do not go onto the next stage until this part of the program is working correctly.

Step 4: putting a picture in the first picture box

SOFTWARE SKILLS
Assigning data to an array

So far we have made the computer select a random number. The next objective will be to display the dog picture if the computer chooses 1 and display a cat picture if the computer chooses 0.

There are two things we need to do:

❯ Assign the dog and cat pictures to elements in the PetNumber array.

❯ Display a picture of either the dog or the cat in picFirst picture box.

To assign the dog and cat pictures there are two lines of code. Here is one of them:

This line of code places the picture of the cat in the 0 element of the PetNumber array, so that PetNumber(0) contains the cat picture.

The line of code for the dog picture works in the same way:

PetNumber (1) = My.Resources.Poppy

Now Petnumber(1) contains the dog picture.

You can look at this line of code as:

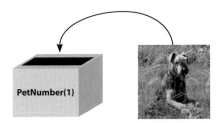

To display the picture of the dog or cat in the picture box there is only one line of code, but it is a line that does a lot! This is the line:

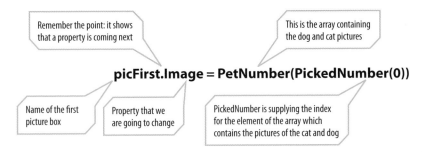

So if **PickedNumber(0)** (the first random number) is **1**, then **PetNumber(1)** (which is the dog picture) is displayed in **picFirst** (the first picture box).

Here is the code that you need to add:

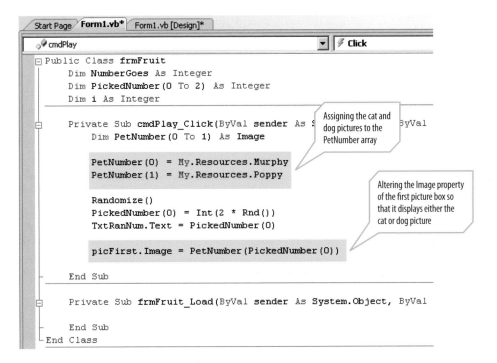

Figure 2.18

Now try it out!

 18   Click the Start Debugging icon on the standard toolbar: ▶

Check that:

> The dog and cat images occur in the position of the first picture box.

> The dog and cat images are random; you may find that several clicks give nothing but one type of picture, but eventually the other picture occurs.

Stage 5: putting images in all three picture boxes

At the moment the game doesn't work because it is not possible to view three pictures in a line across the screen. There are really two problems that we will need to solve:

> The computer will need to put pictures into the remaining two picture boxes.

> The computer will need to be able to count the presses of the play button so that it will put the first picture in the first picture box and the second picture in the second picture box and so on.

Let's start by making the computer count the number of times the Play button is pressed.

We will use the variable NumberGoes to count the button presses. When the program starts, we need to set NumberGoes to 0. The first event to occur is the form's Load event, so this seems a good place to set NumberGoes to 0. The coding is very similar to that we have used previously to assign a value to a variable; in this case the code is:

NumberGoes = 0

Here is the code in the program:

```
Private Sub cmdPlay_Click(ByVal sender As System.Object, ByVal e As
    Dim PetNumber(0 To 1) As Image

    PetNumber(0) = My.Resources.Murphy
    PetNumber(1) = My.Resources.Poppy

    Randomize()
    PickedNumber(0) = Int(2 * Rnd())
    TxtRanNum.Text = PickedNumber(0)

    picF                                     mber(0))

    End Su

    Private Sub frmFruit_Load(ByVal sender As System.Object, ByVal e As
        NumberGoes = 0

    End Sub
End Class
```

> Notice that this is the event handler for the form load event

> Here is the code for setting NumberGoes to 0 while the form loads

Figure 2.19

Now we need to make NumberGoes **increase by one** every time the **Play button is pressed**. See if you can work out how this can be done and discuss your answer with your neighbour.

The answer is to write this code:

NumberGoes = NumberGoes + 1

At first this looks crazy – how can it be true? Well, think of it this way: the 'new' NumberGoes equals the 'old' NumberGoes plus one, so every time this bit of code is run NumberGoes gets increased by one. Simple!

Now think where this bit of code should be placed. If you put it in Form Load, then it will just increase by one when the form loads. We want NumberGoes to increase by one every time the **Play** button is pressed. Does that give you a clue? Well, here's the code:

```
Private Sub cmdPlay_Click(ByVal sender As System.Object, ByVal e As
    Dim PetNumber(0 To 1) As Image

    PetNumber(0) = My.Resources.Murphy
    PetNumber(1) = My.Resources.Poppy

    NumberGoes = NumberGoes + 1

    Randomize()
    PickedNumber(0) = Int(2 * Rnd())
    TxtRanNum.Text = PickedNumber(0)

    picFirst.Image = PetNumber(PickedNumber(0))

End Sub
```

Notice that the code is placed in the event handler for the cmdPlay button. Every press will run the code

Here is the code for increasing NumberGoes by one every time the Play button is pressed

Figure 2.20

Now we need to make pictures of the dog and cat display in the other picture boxes.

To do this we need a piece of code to check the number of times the Play button has been pressed and then put a picture in the correct picture box. If it has been pressed for the first time, then the picture goes in the first picture box; if it is the second time that the button has been pressed, then the picture goes in the second picture box; and so on. This requires a piece of code called a 'selection construct'.

The selection construct looks like a sandwich where **If**, **Then** and **End If** are the slices of bread and the action of the computer is the filling in the middle.

It works like this:

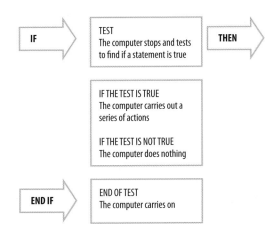

IF → TEST
The computer stops and tests to find if a statement is true → THEN

IF THE TEST IS TRUE
The computer carries out a series of actions

IF THE TEST IS NOT TRUE
The computer does nothing

END IF → END OF TEST
The computer carries on

The instructions for carrying out the selection construct are the words that appear in the arrows in the above diagram; let's see what this looks like in code:

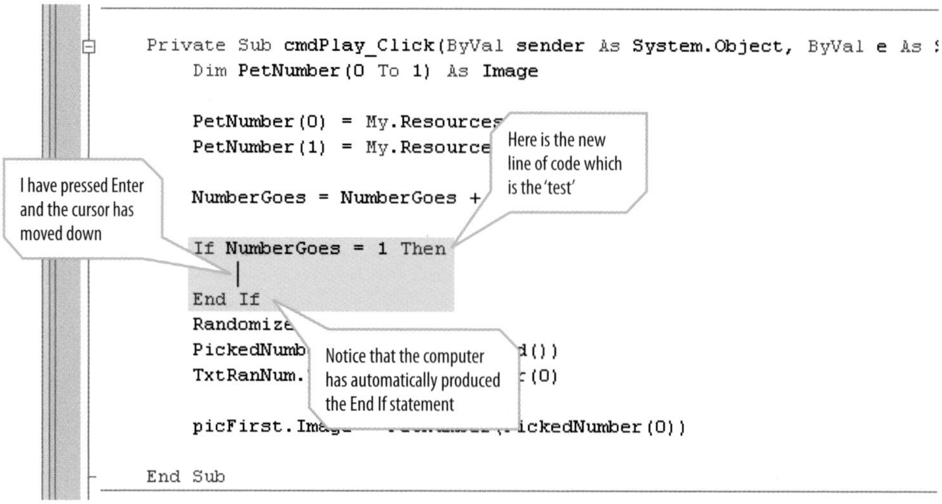

```
Private Sub cmdPlay_Click(ByVal sender As System.Object, ByVal e As S
    Dim PetNumber(O To 1) As Image

    PetNumber(O) = My.Resources
    PetNumber(1) = My.Resource

    NumberGoes = NumberGoes +

    If NumberGoes = 1 Then

    End If
    Randomize
    PickedNumb                              d()
    TxtRanNum.                              (O)

    picFirst.Im           .ickedNumber(O))

End Sub
```

I have pressed Enter and the cursor has moved down

Here is the new line of code which is the 'test'

Notice that the computer has automatically produced the End If statement

Figure 2.21

The problem is that VB has been too helpful this time! It has helpfully added the End If statement, but in the wrong place. All of the remaining code in the cmdPlay needs to be inside the 'sandwich' like this:

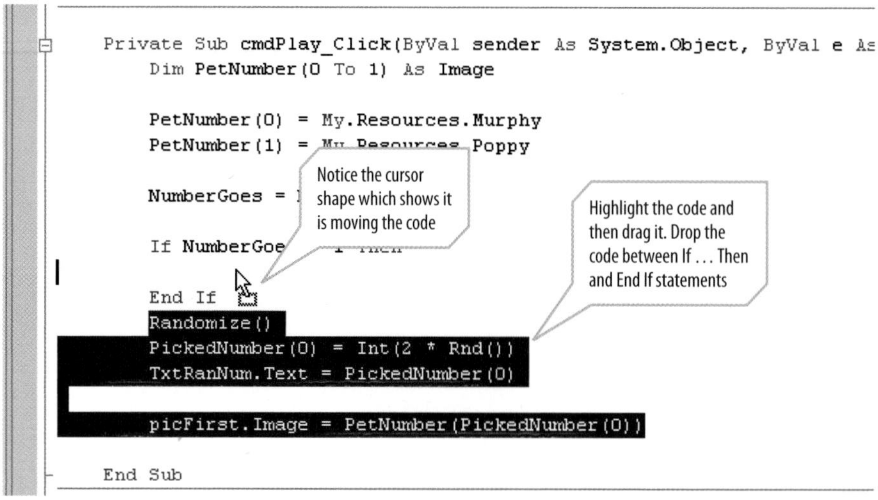

```
Private Sub cmdPlay_Click(ByVal sender As System.Object, ByVal e As
    Dim PetNumber(O To 1) As Image

    PetNumber(O) = My.Resources.Murphy
    PetNumber(1) = My.Resources.Poppy

    NumberGoes =

    If NumberGoe        Then

    End If
    Randomize()
    PickedNumber(O) = Int(2 * Rnd())
    TxtRanNum.Text = PickedNumber(O)

    picFirst.Image = PetNumber(PickedNumber(O))

End Sub
```

Notice the cursor shape which shows it is moving the code

Highlight the code and then drag it. Drop the code between If ... Then and End If statements

Figure 2.22

Now check Figure 2.23 to make sure that your have dragged/dropped the code into the correct place.

```
Private Sub cmdPlay_Click(ByVal sender As System.Object, ByVal e As
    Dim PetNumber(0 To 1) As Image

    PetNumber(0) = My.Resources.Murphy
    PetNumber(1) = My.Resources.Poppy

    NumberGoes = NumberGoes + 1

    If NumberGoes = 1 Then
        Randomize()
        PickedNumber(0) = Int(2 * Rnd())
        TxtRanNum.Text = PickedNumber(0)

        picFirst.Image = PetNumber(PickedNumber(0))
    End If

End Sub
```

> Here is the code in place (just click anywhere to remove the highlight)

Figure 2.23

 19 Try running the program.

Do you notice that only one picture is displayed? Can you work out a reason for this?

There are two answers:

➤ When you click cmdPlay, a picture appears in the first picture box. More clicks do not change the picture because the IF statement will reject them as untrue since NumberGoes does not equal 1. (Remember that NumberGoes increases by one every time you click the play button.)

➤ Pictures do not occur in the other text boxes because we have not written any code to put them there. Computers can't guess what you want them to do!

We need to write code to place pictures in the remaining picture boxes. If you think about this, the code will be very similar to that we have just written, except:

➤ It will refer to a different picture box.

➤ The box that the picture goes in will depend on the number of times the play button has been pressed, that is the number stored in the variable NumberGoes.

OK, let's get cloning code!

 20 Highlight all of the **If… Then… End If** construct like this:

```
    NumberGoes = NumberGoes + 1

    If NumberGoes = 1 Then
        Randomize()
        PickedNumber(0) = Int(2 * Rnd())
        TxtRanNum.Text = PickedNumber(0)

        picFirst.Image = PetNumber(PickedNumber(0))
    End If

End Sub
```

Figure 2.24

Now hold down the **Ctrl** key on your keyboard and press the **C** key to copy the selected code. Nothing appears to happen.

 Place your cursor beneath **End If** (make another empty line by pressing Enter if necessary).

 Hold down the **Ctrl key** again and press the **V key** to paste the code.

Success! The copied code appears under the 'old' selection construct. We need another copy, so:

 Check that you have the cursor in an empty line under the last **End If** statement, then paste in another copy.

Check you haven't been too enthusiastic! There should be three selection constructs as shown in Figure 2.25:

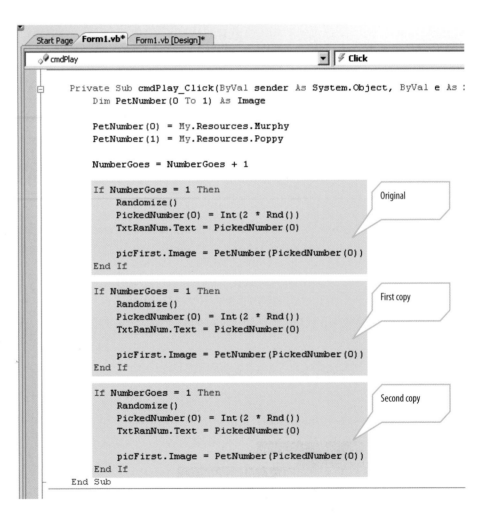

Figure 2.25

For the first copy you need to make some changes to the copied code so that it selects on the second click of cmdPlay and then loads a new picture of either a dog or a cat into picSecond. Figure 2.26 shows the changes that are needed.

```
        If NumberGoes = 1 Then
            Randomize()
            PickedNumber(0) = Int(2 * Rnd())
            TxtRanNum.Text = PickedNumber(0)

            p:        Image = PetNumber(PickedNumber(0))
        End If

        If NumberGoes = 2 Th
            Randomize()
            PickedNumber(1) = Int(2 * Rnd())
            TxtRanNum.Text = PickedNumber(1)

            picSecond.Image = PetNumber(PickedNumber(1))
        End If

        If NumberGoes          n
            Randomize(
            PickedNumber(0) = Int(2 * Rnd())
            TxtRanNum.Text = PickedNumber(0)

            picFirst.Image = PetNumber(PickedNumber(0))
        End If
    End Sub
```

Change
Change
Change
Change
Change

Figure 2.26

Now it's just a matter of making similar changes for the last selection construct.

```
        If NumberGoes = 1 Then
            Randomize()
            PickedNumber(0) = Int(2 * Rnd())
            TxtRanNum.Text = PickedNumber(0)

            picFirst.Image = PetNumber(PickedNumber(0))
        End If

        If NumberGoes = 2 Then
            Randomize()
            PickedNumber(1) = Int(2 * Rnd())
            TxtRanNum.Text = PickedNumber(1)

            p:        .Image = PetNumber(PickedNumber(1))
        End If

        If NumberGoes = 3 Th
            Randomize()
            PickedNumber(2) = Int(2 * Rnd())
            TxtRanNum.Text = PickedNumber(2)

            picThird.Image = PetNumber(PickedNumber(2))
        End If
    End Sub
```

Change
Change
Change
Change
Change

Figure 2.27

Well, it's the moment of truth! Give the code a final check and then run the program.

Notice that the program appears to stop after the third press of the Play button: but you would expect this wouldn't you?

That's it, sit back and enjoy the game!

Oh … just remember to **Save All** before you go! 🖫

There remain a few tiding jobs we can do and it would be nice to supply a restart button and a pop-up for the winning line of dogs or cats; but we will leave these for the next task.

GET AHEAD

We are not finished with this project and the next task will add more functionality to it, but you may want to put your own 'stamp' on the GUI, so here a few ideas to get you started:

 Change the colour of the form or you might like to try applying a background image by using this facility in the properties for the form. The Background Image property will guide you to bringing in another picture to your Resources folder.

 Change the colour, shape and size of the fonts used on the buttons so that the game is visible from some distance.

 You could alter the size of the form by changing its properties; you may need to reposition the controls on the form.

 Here's something for you to puzzle about: we want to be able to run the fruit machine several times without having to reload the program each time. How could we arrange this, what extra control(s) will we need and what will have to happen at the end of each game before the next game starts?

 Try and find some information on early uses of the computer. Try looking up Alan Turing, Bletchley Park and Enigma. Use the information to make a poster on breaking secret codes. Here is a useful site on one of the machines built to crack secret code, 'Colossus':

http://www.codesandciphers.org.uk/lorenz/rebuild.htm

CHECKPOINT

Check that you know how to:

➤ Declare a local and global variable

➤ Declare an array

➤ Assign data to an element of an array

➤ Make the computer count the number of button presses

➤ Write a selection construct

➤ Copy, paste and move code

➤ Edit code

ASSESSMENT POINT

Now let's assess the work. Look back at the table at the beginning of this section (**Target point**) and decide on which of the statements you can answer 'Yes' to.

Did you do as well as you expected? Could you improve your work? Use Word to write a comment to show what you could do to improve your work and remember this when starting your next ICT project.

TASK BRIEF

In this task you will complete the fruit machine game.

By the end of Task 2 you had a basic working version of the fruit machine and you may have carried out some 'customising' of its appearance as suggested in the Get Ahead section of Task 2, but there are some remaining problems to solve before it is a suitable program for the user; for example, not being able to run the game again and again without having to reload the program each time.

The table below shows the problems requiring our attention and how we will solve them:

Steps	Problem	Solution	New VB controls	New VB code needed
1	No automatic reloading at the end of a game	Make the program reset by emptying the text box and picture boxes	Provide a new button to reset the program	Emptying the text and picture boxes Resetting the go counter to zero
2	Nothing to show you have won a game	Make the program display a 'Win' message for a winning line of three similar pets	Provide a new text box to insert a 'Win' message	Checking whether a win has occurred (three similar pictures) Displaying a winning message
3	The player can't select the number of times they wish to play	Allow the player to set the number of turns they wish to play	Provide a new NumericUpDown control which can be used to select the number of turns	Counting the number of turns Stopping the program once the number of turns is completed
4	The game can only be used on the computer that built it and it is difficult to start the program running	Make the program into an executable file. This means the program runs on any computer, even if it doesn't have the software that built the program on it	None required	No new code to be written but we will use the Publish Wizard to collect together the code that is needed

Being able to just click the game's icon on a menu without loading VB would be great!

SOFTWARE SKILLS

You will learn how to:

- ❯ Use and understand a loop
- ❯ Use a NumericUpDown control
- ❯ Use the Enabled property to control the access to buttons
- ❯ Convert the program into an executable file

FUNCTIONAL SKILLS

As you work through this task the Functional Skills tabs will explain to you why the task tackles the brief in the way shown here and explain why you would choose to:

- ❯ Create a design that is suitable for your target audience
- ❯ Test the program's functionality
- ❯ Publish your program

CAPABILITY

You are not expected to show capability in this Task because you are following a set of instructions, although if you complete the Get Ahead section you will be working on your own and therefore will be showing capability in changing and adding images, and solving problems involving a For… To… Next loop and a new text control.

VOCABULARY

You should learn these new words and understand what they mean.

- ❯ Loop (For… To… Next)
- ❯ NumericUpDown control
- ❯ Executable file

RESOURCES

These are the resources for this task:

Your VB project from Task 2

A copy of the project completed up to this point is available from www.payne-gallway.co.uk

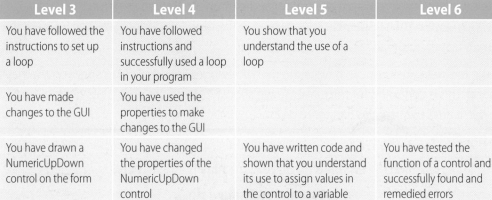

	Level 3	Level 4	Level 5	Level 6
	You have followed the instructions to set up a loop	You have followed instructions and successfully used a loop in your program	You show that you understand the use of a loop	
	You have made changes to the GUI	You have used the properties to make changes to the GUI		
	You have drawn a NumericUpDown control on the form	You have changed the properties of the NumericUpDown control	You have written code and shown that you understand its use to assign values in the control to a variable	You have tested the function of a control and successfully found and remedied errors
	You have followed the instructions to convert the program to an executable file	You have successfully converted the program to an executable file	You have shown that you understand the benefits of converting the program to an exectable file	
	You have followed the instructions to write a loop		You have successfully incorporated a loop into the code of the program	You have shown that you understand the use of a For… To… Next loop in the program

TARGET POINT

Have a look at the following statements before you start your task so you know what you are aiming for.

Although you will not make your own decisions on the design of the program in Task 2, you can use what you learn here to help with other work that will be awarded a particular level.

OK, let's get started.

 Open **Visual Basic 2008 Express Edition** as you did for the previous tasks.

 Once VB has loaded, in the **Recent Projects** pane, click **Fruit Machine** (or the file name you used for the Task 2 project); see Figure 3.1.

Figure 3.1

When the program has loaded check that it runs correctly by clicking on the **Start Debugging** icon ▷ on the standard toolbar.

Run the program several times to make sure that both of the pictures are used in the program and that images occur in all three picture boxes.

If all is well … on with solving the problems. We'll deal with each one listed in the table in turn.

SOLVING PROBLEMS WITH THE GAME
Step 1: making the program restart

This is a major problem with the program at the moment. Having to re-run the program every time we want it to play is a serious fault in the program design. Let's see how we can make it restart automatically.

At the moment, the user can have more than three goes by just clicking again on the Play button. This is confusing for the player so we should change the properties of cmdPlay to disable it after the user has had three goes.

Any ideas?

What about resetting the **Enabled** property of the **Play** button to **False** by using this code?

cmdPlay.Enabled = False

This would mean that the button would appear greyed-out, the user would see that their turn had finished and it would also have the effect that the user **couldn't** click the button!

It seems a good idea, but where should we place this code? If we were to place it too early in the cmdPlay event handler, the game would stop too soon, so it must be placed just after the last go has ended, as you can see in Figure 3.2.

Type in the new code as shown in Figure 3.2.

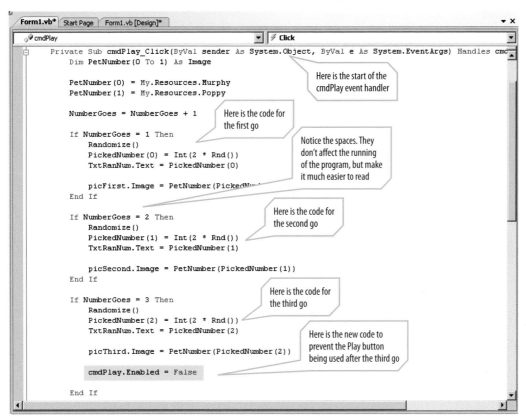

```
Form1.vb*   Start Page   Form1.vb [Design]*                                              ▾ ✕
cmdPlay                                               ▾  Click                                          ▾
     Private Sub cmdPlay_Click(ByVal sender As System.Object, ByVal e As System.EventArgs) Handles cmd
         Dim PetNumber(0 To 1) As Image

         PetNumber(0) = My.Resources.Murphy
         PetNumber(1) = My.Resources.Poppy

         NumberGoes = NumberGoes + 1

         If NumberGoes = 1 Then
             Randomize()
             PickedNumber(0) = Int(2 * Rnd())
             TxtRanNum.Text = PickedNumber(0)

             picFirst.Image = PetNumber(PickedN
         End If

         If NumberGoes = 2 Then
             Randomize()
             PickedNumber(1) = Int(2 * Rnd())
             TxtRanNum.Text = PickedNumber(1)

             picSecond.Image = PetNumber(PickedNumber(1))
         End If

         If NumberGoes = 3 Then
             Randomize()
             PickedNumber(2) = Int(2 * Rnd())
             TxtRanNum.Text = PickedNumber(2)

             picThird.Image = PetNumber(PickedNumber(2))

             cmdPlay.Enabled = False

         End If
```

> Here is the start of the cmdPlay event handler

> Here is the code for the first go

> Notice the spaces. They don't affect the running of the program, but make it much easier to read

> Here is the code for the second go

> Here is the code for the third go

> Here is the new code to prevent the Play button being used after the third go

Figure 3.2

 Now try it out by running the program.

After the third go, the play button is clearly not working:

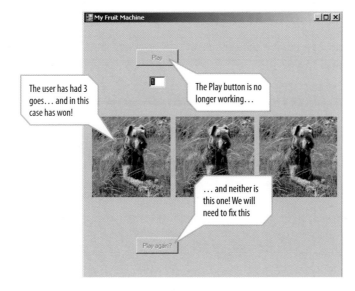

> The user has had 3 goes... and in this case has won!

> The Play button is no longer working...

> ... and neither is this one! We will need to fix this

Figure 3.3

At the moment, the Play again button is not useable. Originally we set the properties for this button to Enabled = False so that it was obvious to the user that the button was not to be clicked during their turn. Now that their turn has ended, we want to be able to use the button to start another turn, so we will need to change the property Enabled to **True**. Make sure that the program is **not running**, then swap to viewing the code by clicking the **View Code** icon ▤ on the **Solution Explorer**, or double click on the form.

Can you think of the code we need to make the button enabled again, and where should this code be placed?

Here's the code:

cmdAgain.Enabled = True

and the code needs to be placed in the Play button at the end of the third go so that, as the **Play** button is 'turned off', the **Play again?** button is 'turned on'.

 Type the new code into the event handler for cmdPlay:

```
If NumberGoes = 3 Then
    Randomize()
    PickedNumber(2) = Int(2 * Rnd())
    TxtRanNum.Text = PickedNumber(2)

    picThird.Image = PetNumber(PickedNumber(2))

    cmdPlay.Enabled = False
    cmdAgain.Enabled = True

    End If
End Sub
```

This is the code in cmdPlay that handles the third go

Here is the code that turns on the Play again? button

Figure 3.4

 Run the program again to check that the Play again? button is working.

The button won't do anything of course; it doesn't have any code in its event handler.

That's better – the button is ready to work

Figure 3.5

Well, that seems to work. What's next?

Now that it is available, it would be a good idea to use the **Play Again?** button to set the **Enabled** property for the **Play** button to **True**.

This would mean that the user would have their first turn of three goes and then if they wanted another turn (remember they would need to pay again for another three goes), they would click the Play again? button, which would make the Play button work. The code for this will be very similar to that we have just used – can you think of the code and work out where to put it?

OK, this is the code:

cmdPlay.Enabled = True

And it needs to go in the event handler for the cmdAgain button as you can see in Figure 3.6.

 Type the new code into the event handler for cmdAgain:

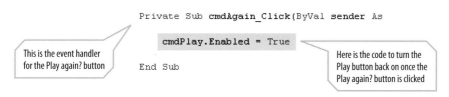

```
Private Sub cmdAgain_Click(ByVal sender As

        cmdPlay.Enabled = True

End Sub
```

This is the event handler for the Play again? button

Here is the code to turn the Play button back on once the Play again? button is clicked

Figure 3.6

> **TIP**
>
> *You will find that the event handler for cmdAgain is not displayed in View Code unless you double click the Play again? button in design view.*
>
> *Once you have done this, VB will 'remember' that cmdAgain is important to the program and always show the cmdAgain event handler in View Code.*

Step 2: setting the number of goes back to zero

For another turn to take place, the number of goes must be reset to zero.

SOFTWARE SKILLS
Using code to reset a variable

Up to now this has happened because, as the form loads, there is already code in the form_load event handler that sets the value in the variable NumberGoes to zero. However, if we want to re-run the game without reloading the program, we have to write code to reset the value in the variable to zero after each run because at the moment the form only loads once, when the program loads.

Before we write the code we need to answer two questions:

> What is the code?

> Where does the code go in the program?

Any ideas? It's important to have a think about these questions – you have the experience to answer them correctly and eventually you need to write your own code and not follow these instructions as a 'recipe'.

Here's the code:

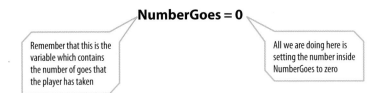

NumberGoes = 0

Remember that this is the variable which contains the number of goes that the player has taken

All we are doing here is setting the number inside NumberGoes to zero

Now to answer the second question: the code will obviously have to go after a turn of three goes has ended. The best place for the code would be in the Play again? button event handler because that way NumberGoes is set to zero ready for the start of the next turn.

 Type the new code into the event handler for cmdAgain:

```
Private Sub cmdAgain_Click(ByVal sender As

    cmdPlay.Enabled = True
    NumberGoes = 0

End Sub
```

Here is the code to set to zero the number stored in the variable NumberGoes

Figure 3.7

But how do we know if the code works?

Well that's easy – we'll make a temporary text box which will display the number in NumberGoes.

 Draw another text box on the form.

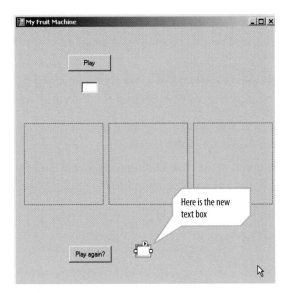

Here is the new text box

Figure 3.8

8 In the properties for the new text box, change its name to:

txtGoesTest

Figure 3.9

Now we need some code to write the contents of NumberGoes into the text property of the new text box.

Here's the code:

txtGoesTest.Text = NumberGoes

As you would expect the code is placed in the Play again? event handler:

 9 Type the new code into the event handler for cmdAgain:

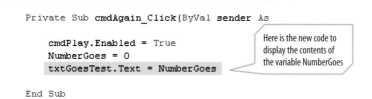

Figure 3.10

While we are making the game it would be useful to see the value in NumberGoes increasing as the game is played, in other words showing a count of the number of goes that a player has had. This will help to check that our program is working correctly.

Once the game is complete we'll delete the text box and the code that it uses because, when you think about it, it's obvious how many goes the player has had – the number of pictures gives you a good clue!

SOFTWARE SKILLS
Using Copy and Paste to replicate code

10 Copy the new code (look back at Task 2 if you can't remember how to copy code).

11 Paste the new code into the Play button event handler as shown in Figure 3.11.

```
Private Sub cmdPlay_Click(ByVal sender As
    Dim PetNumber(0 To 1) As Image

    PetNumber(0) = My.Resources.Murphy
    PetNumber(1) = My.Resources.Poppy

    NumberGoes = NumberGoes + 1
    txtGoesTest.Text = NumberGoes

    If NumberGoes = 1 Then
        Randomize()
        PickedNumber(0) = Int(2 * Rnd())
        TxtRanNum.Text = PickedNumber(0)
```

> Here is the new code copied and pasted into the cmdPlay event handler

Figure 3.11

Why have we copied the code into here? Think about it this way: every time the Play button is clicked, its event handler will run. Each time the code reaches

NumberGoes = NumberGoes + 1

the value stored in NumberGoes is increased by one. This value is displayed in txtGoesTest.

Try it out!

12 Run the program and click through three goes. You should see the number in the bottom text box increase each time the Play button is pressed and return to zero once the Play again? button is pressed.

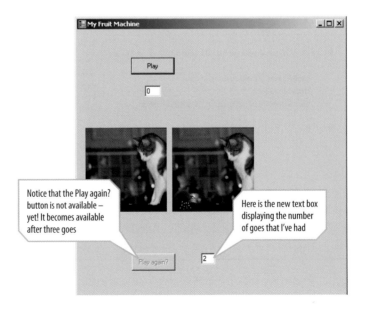

> Notice that the Play again? button is not available – yet! It becomes available after three goes

> Here is the new text box displaying the number of goes that I've had

Figure 3.12

Step 3: emptying the text and picture boxes

When the user starts another turn, the picture boxes need to empty of their dog and cat images. The text box showing the random number that has been chosen (txtRanNum) also has to be emptied.

The code for doing this for picture boxes is:

pictureBoxName.image = Nothing

and for text boxes is:

textBoxName.text = ""

Although the methods are different for the picture and text boxes, it is fairly obvious what is going on. The problem is where to put this code – any ideas?

Well, you couldn't place it in the event handler for the Play button because every time the button was clicked it would wipe out the pictures from the previous goes. What about putting it in the event handler for the Play again? button? If you did that, would that reset the picture boxes and text box ready for the next turn?

Of course the answer is yes. The new code is shown in place in Figure 3.13.

 Type the new code into the event handler for cmdAgain:

```
Private Sub cmdAgain_Click(ByVal sender As

    cmdPlay.Enabled = True
    NumberGoes = 0
    txtGoesTest.Text = NumberGoes

    picFirst.Image  = Nothing
    picSecond.Image = Nothing
    picThird.Image  = Nothing

    TxtRanNum.Text = ""

End Sub
```

> Here is the new code. Remember that when entering code, you can accept what VB offers by pressing the tab key

Figure 3.13

 Try out the new code by running the program.

Stop the program and return to the code view.

MAKING CHANGES TO THE GUI

Displaying a winning message is not strictly needed, but would be a nice addition and make the game look a little more 'professional'. It's easy to do – all we need is to check that the pictures are all the same and, if they are, to display a winning message.

Step 1: make a new text box

A new text box will be needed to display the 'Win!' message; let's do this first.

 First of all swap to the design view and draw the new text box onto the form:

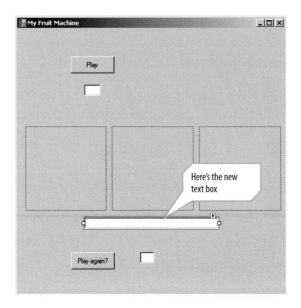

Figure 3.14

Step 2: set the properties for the new text box

Now we need to set the properties for the new text box – see the table below:

Type of object	Property to change	Setting	Reason
Text box	Name	txtWin	Unique name for the text box
	Font	Bauhaus93	Choose a font that you like!
		Size 24	Choose a font size that does not make the text box overlap other objects on the form
	Location	125, 335	Position on the form
	Locked	True	Stops the user from moving or resizing the control
	Size	245, 54	This is a guide and will depend on the size of font that you set

 Change the **Font** property – click the current font and then the ellipsis (three dots) that appears:

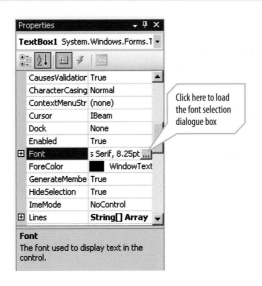

Figure 3.15

Use the font selection dialogue box to allow you to select an alternative font, weight and size:

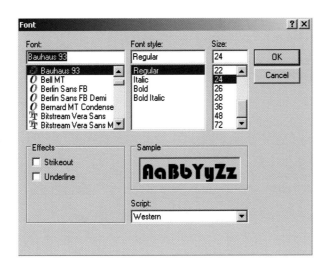

Figure 3.16

Step 3: code

Now we need to add code that will cause the 'Win' message to be displayed. The text box that displays the name of the game will change colour and display the winning message.

The code for this looks like the following:

	Code	Purpose
If	PickedNumber(0) = PickedNumber(1) And PickedNumber(0) = PickedNumber(2) Then	Test
	txtWin.Text = "Win!"	What happens if the test is true
	txtWin.Backcolor = Color.Red	
Else	txtWin.Text = ("Fruit Machine")	What happens if the test is not true
End If		End of construct

You could, of course, write your own name instead of 'Fruit Machine' and make the BackColor another colour.

Now that we understand the code, we need to decide where it should be placed. The new code should be in the event handler for the Play button because then the computer can check whether all three random numbers are the same.

Here is a view of the new code added to the event handler for the Play button:

```
If NumberGoes = 3 Then
    Randomize()
    PickedNumber(2) = Int(2 * Rnd())
    TxtRanNum.Text = PickedNumber(2)

    picThird.Image = PetNumber(PickedNumber(2))

    cmdPlay.Enabled = False
    cmdAgain.Enabled = True

End If


If PickedNumber(0) = PickedNumber(1) And PickedNumber(0) = PickedNumber(2) Then

    txtWin.Text = ("Win!")
    txtWin.BackColor = Color.Red
Else : txtWin.Text = ("Fruit machine")

End If

End Sub
```

> Here is the code already typed into the cmdPlay event handler; this is shown just to give you an idea where to place the new code

> This is the new code

Figure 3.17

 19 Type the new code into the cmdPlay event handler.

Step 4: troubleshooting

Whoops!

If you try running the program you will probably find that, although the game works, the text in the txtWin text box is not always relevant, sometimes telling you there is a win even though only one picture is displayed!

This can be dealt with by resetting the PickedNumber array using a **For... To... Next** loop. Using the global variable i (see p. 58) this code loops through each element in the array in turn. Here is the code to clear the previous turn's random numbers shown in place in the event handler cmdAgain:

```
Private Sub frmFruit_Load(ByVal sender As System.Object, ByVal e As
    NumberGoes = 0

    For i = 0 To 2
        PickedNumber(i) = i

    Next
End Sub

Private Sub cmdAgain_Click(ByVal send    As System.Object, ByVal e As

    cmdPlay.Enabled = True
    NumberGoes = 0
    txtGoesTest.Text = NumberGoes

    picFirst.Image = Nothing
    picSecond.Image = Nothing
    picThird.Image = Nothing

    TxtRanNum.Text = ""

    For i = 0 To 2
        PickedNumber(i) = i
    Next

    End Sub
End Class
```

2. And here is the same code being used to set the values stored in the PickedNumber array to different values as the form loads for the first game

1. Here is the new code to set the values stored in the PickedNumber array to different values

Figure 3.18

 20 Write in the code as shown in Figure 3.18 and then copy it into the event handler for frmFruit.

Another annoyance is that the red background does not reset for the next turn after a win and the 'Win!' message doesn't clear until the next turn starts. This fixes it:

```
Private Sub cmdAgain_Click(ByVal sender As

    cmdPlay.Enabled = True
    NumberGoes = 0
    txtGoesTest.Text = NumberGoes

    picFirst.Image = Nothing
    picSecond.Image = Nothing
    picThird.Image = Nothing

    TxtRanNum.Text = ""

    For i = 0 To 2
        PickedNumber(i) = i
    Next

    txtWin.BackColor = Color.White
    txtWin.Text = ("Ready")

    End Sub
```

Notice that the code to reset txtWin is in the event handler for cmdAgain, so that this code is executed when the Play again? button is clicked

This code turns the BackColor to white ready for the next turn and inserts the message 'Ready' to show that the program is ready for another turn

Figure 3.19

 21 Try running the program.

ENABLING THE PLAYER TO SELECT THE NUMBER OF TURNS

Quite often, players would prefer to buy a number of turns rather than pay for individual turns. This means that we will have to devise a way of enabling the players to select the number of turns that they require and then making the program respond so that they are allowed their turns and no more.

We are going to use a NumericUpDown control to enable the players to select their turns.

Step 1: make changes to the GUI

 If the program is still running, stop it and then return to the design view.

 Click on the **NumericUpDown** icon in the toolbox…

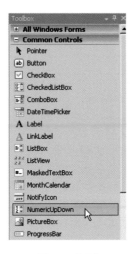

Figure 3.20

… and draw a box with it on the form:

Figure 3.21

It is a good time to reorganise the GUI. The idea of this is to change the position of the Play again? and Play buttons. The buttons are locked in place so the easiest way to do this is through changing the properties in the next step.

Step 2: set the properties

We need to set the properties for the new control and redesign the GUI so that the cmdAgain event handler becomes a 'Ready' button which is clicked before each turn.

SOFTWARE SKILLS
Resetting properties after changes to the interface

 Now set the properties as in the table; **be careful here** – some of the settings for the buttons have changed and, if you miss them, the program will not work correctly!

Type of object	Property to change	Setting	Reason
NumericUpDown	Name	udnTurns	Unique name for the control
	Font	Microsoft Sans Serif Size 10	Choose a font size that is big enough to be seen but not out of keeping with the rest of the GUI
	Location	350, 75	Position on the form
	Locked	True	Stops the user from moving or resizing the control
	Size	40,22	This is a guide and will depend on the size of font that you set
Button	Name	cmdAgain	Unique name for the control
	Enabled	True	This button needs to available to the player as soon as the program loads
	Location	100, 75	Position on the form
	Locked	True	Stops the user from moving or resizing the control
	Size	100, 35	
	Text	Ready?	New text showing the slight change in use of the button
Button	Name	cmdPlay	Unique name for the control
	Location	100, 420	Position on the form
	Locked	True	Stops the user from moving or resizing the control
	Size	100, 35	
	Text	Play	
Text box	Name	txtWin	Unique name for the control
	Font	Bauhaus93 Size 24	You could use another suitable font, but you will find that the size of the text box will change
	Location	250, 420	Position on the form
	Locked	True	Stops the user from moving or resizing the control
	Size	325, 54	The actual size will be set by the size of font
	TabIndex	0	Avoids the cursor appearing in the text box at the end of a turn

Step 3: make changes to the code

The way this works is simple.

The NumericUpDown control will be used by the player to set the number of turns that they want. The value in the NumericUpDown is then stored in a variable which is decreased by one every turn taken by the player. When the value stored in the variable reaches zero, code is used to switch off the Play and the Play again? buttons so that no further turns are possible.

This variable needs to be used by several parts of the program and is therefore a global variable. Check with Task 2 if you can't remember how to set up a global variable.

First of all let's set up the variable.

 Type in the code as shown in Figure 3.22.

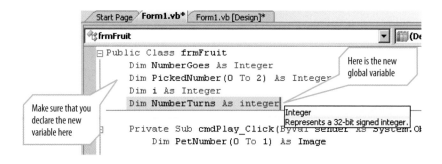

Figure 3.22

Now we need some code to assign the value that the player has set in the NumericUpDown control. This is straightforward, but remember to read from *right* to *left*:

NumberTurns = udnTurns.Value

| Variable | Assigning | Name of NumericUpDown control | Value set by user in the control |

Figure 3.23 shows the code in place; notice that it is in the cmdAgain event handler. You can see why it should be placed here; this button re-sets the game before every turn.

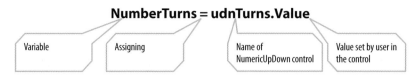

```
Private Sub cmdAgain_Click(ByVal sender As

    NumberTurns = udnTurns.Value
```

Figure 3.23

 Type in the code as shown in Figure 3.23.

This code assigns the value of the NumericUpDown control to the new variable.

Now we need to reduce the value stored in NumberTurns by one for every turn taken. The code for this is similar to what we have used before to count the number of goes, but of course we are counting down and not up!

NumberTurns = NumberTurns – 1

 Type the code as shown in Figure 3.24 into the cmdPlay event handler.

```
If NumberGoes = 3 Then
    Randomize()
    PickedNumber(2) = Int(2 * Rnd())
    TxtRanNum.Text = PickedNumber(2)

    picThird.Image = PetNumber(Picke

    cmdPlay.Enabled = False
    cmdAgain.Enabled = True

    NumberTurns = NumberTurns - 1
    udnTurns.Value = NumberTurns

End If


If PickedNumber(0) = PickedNumber(             (0) = PickedNumber(2) Then

    txtWin.Text = ("Win!")
    txtWin.BackColor = Color.Red
Else : txtWin.Text = ("Fruit machine")

End If

End Sub
```

> This is the select construct for the third picture in the cmdPlay event handler

> Here is the 'countdown' code for the number of turns

> Here is another line of code which has been added to update the NumericUpDown control with the number of remaining turns

Figure 3.24

Step 4: test the program
Play the game for three turns.

 Try running the program. You need to run it by clicking on the **Start Debugging** icon as usual: ▶

 As soon as the program loads select 3 in the NumericUpDown control, then click the **Read?** button:

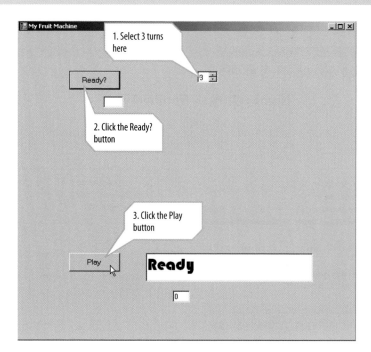

Figure 3.25

Success! Start celebrations…

Not so fast.

 Now try a *fourth* turn – after all, there is nothing to stop you!

As soon as you make the third click for the last picture: CRASH!

Step 5: debug the program

The problem is the variable NumberTurns now contains –1, which it has attempted to transfer to udnTurns. A NumericUpDown control cannot contain a negative number, hence the crash!

 Type the new code into the cmdPlay event handler.

```
If PickedNumber(0) = PickedNumber(1) And PickedNumber(0) = PickedNumber(2) Then
    txtWin.Text = ("Win!")
    txtWin.BackColor = Color.Red
Else : txtWin.Text = ("Fruit machine")

End If

If NumberTurns > 0 Then
    cmdPlay.Enabled = True
Else : cmdPlay.Enabled = False
    cmdAgain.Enabled = False

End If

End Sub
```

Here is the selection construct for the winning display. It's shown so that you can see where to place the new code

Here is the new code, which prevents access to the buttons if the turns are finished

Figure 3.26

 Test the program.

 Stop the program and return to design view.

Step 6: tidying up the loading of the program

We need both to protect the program from the player pressing buttons in the wrong order and to show the player how to play the game.

 If necessary, swap to design view.

 Double click on the form.

 Enter this code into the frmFruit event handler.

```
Private Sub frmFruit_Load(ByVal sender As System.Object, ByVal e As
    NumberGoes = 0
    cmdAgain.Enabled = False
    cmdPlay.Enabled = False


    For i = 0 To 2
        PickedNumber(i) = i

    Next

End Sub
```

Figure 3.27

If you can't see what this does, just try running the program. Did you get very far?

Well that has made the program very safe, but of no use. We need a way to make the Ready button become available at the very start of the game. The way to do this is to make it available once the player has entered their number of turns; we'll try that next.

 If necessary, swap to design view.

 Double click on the NumericUpDown control.

 Enter this code in the udnTurns event handler. We have used code like this before – see if you can work out what it does and why it is necessary.

```
Private Sub udnTurns_ValueChanged(ByVal sender As System.Object, ByVal e As

    If udnTurns.Value > 0 Then
        cmdAgain.Enabled = True
    End If

    End Sub
-End Class
```

Figure 3.28

 Try running the program again.

This time you have to use the **NumericUpDown** control to start the game and make the 'Ready?' button available.

41 Save your work by clicking the **Save All** button 🖫 on the standard toolbar.

The **txtRanNum** and **txtGoesTest** text boxes are not needed, so we will remove all of the code that refers to them and then remove the text boxes themselves. Do it this way round otherwise VB will get lost running around looking for the deleted text boxes!

42 Delete the code shown in the highlighted boxes in Figures 3.29 and 3.30.

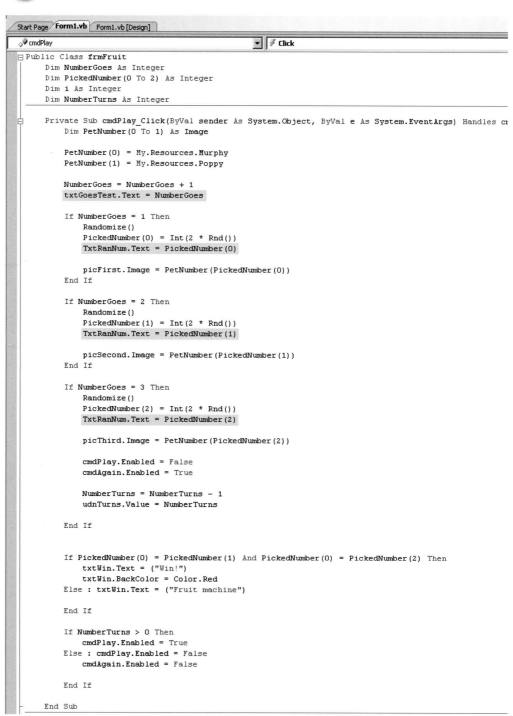

```vb
Start Page   Form1.vb   Form1.vb [Design]
cmdPlay                                              Click

Public Class frmFruit
    Dim NumberGoes As Integer
    Dim PickedNumber(0 To 2) As Integer
    Dim i As Integer
    Dim NumberTurns As Integer

    Private Sub cmdPlay_Click(ByVal sender As System.Object, ByVal e As System.EventArgs) Handles cm
        Dim PetNumber(0 To 1) As Image

        PetNumber(0) = My.Resources.Murphy
        PetNumber(1) = My.Resources.Poppy

        NumberGoes = NumberGoes + 1
        txtGoesTest.Text = NumberGoes

        If NumberGoes = 1 Then
            Randomize()
            PickedNumber(0) = Int(2 * Rnd())
            TxtRanNum.Text = PickedNumber(0)

            picFirst.Image = PetNumber(PickedNumber(0))
        End If

        If NumberGoes = 2 Then
            Randomize()
            PickedNumber(1) = Int(2 * Rnd())
            TxtRanNum.Text = PickedNumber(1)

            picSecond.Image = PetNumber(PickedNumber(1))
        End If

        If NumberGoes = 3 Then
            Randomize()
            PickedNumber(2) = Int(2 * Rnd())
            TxtRanNum.Text = PickedNumber(2)

            picThird.Image = PetNumber(PickedNumber(2))

            cmdPlay.Enabled = False
            cmdAgain.Enabled = True

            NumberTurns = NumberTurns - 1
            udnTurns.Value = NumberTurns

        End If


        If PickedNumber(0) = PickedNumber(1) And PickedNumber(0) = PickedNumber(2) Then
            txtWin.Text = ("Win!")
            txtWin.BackColor = Color.Red
        Else : txtWin.Text = ("Fruit machine")

        End If

        If NumberTurns > 0 Then
            cmdPlay.Enabled = True
        Else : cmdPlay.Enabled = False
            cmdAgain.Enabled = False

        End If

    End Sub
```

Figure 3.29

```
Start Page | Form1.vb | Form1.vb [Design]

cmdPlay                                          | Click

    Private Sub frmFruit_Load(ByVal sender As System.Object, ByVal e As System.EventArgs) Handles MyB
        NumberGoes = 0
        cmdAgain.Enabled = False
        cmdPlay.Enabled = False


        For i = 0 To 2
            PickedNumber(i) = i

        Next

    End Sub

    Private Sub cmdAgain_Click(ByVal sender As System.Object, ByVal e As System.EventArgs) Handles cm

        NumberTurns = udnTurns.Value

        cmdPlay.Enabled = True
        NumberGoes = 0
        txtGoesTest.Text = NumberGoes

        picFirst.Image = Nothing
        picSecond.Image = Nothing
        picThird.Image = Nothing

        TxtRanNum.Text = ""

        For i = 0 To 2
            PickedNumber(i) = i
        Next

        txtWin.BackColor = Color.White
        txtWin.Text = ("Ready")

    End Sub

    Private Sub udnTurns_ValueChanged(ByVal sender As System.Object, ByVal e As System.EventArgs) Han

        If udnTurns.Value > 0 Then
            cmdAgain.Enabled = True
        End If

    End Sub
End Class
```

Figure 3.30

 Now swap to the design view and delete the **txtRanNum** and **txtGoesTest** text boxes.

 Test the program and, if all is well, save the program by clicking the **Save All** icon on the standard toolbar:

SOFTWARE SKILLS
Creating an executable file

FUNCTIONAL SKILLS
Publishing your program – you should publish your program in a way that makes it easily accessible for your users; for example, as an .exe file so that they don't need to install the VB software

PUBLISHING THE PROGRAM AS AN EXECUTABLE FILE

At the moment we can only run the program within VB 2008. If a computer does not have this program installed on its hard drive, then we will be unable to run the program; but VB 2008 offers a way around this problem by giving us the opportunity to 'Publish' the program.

Once we have done this, the program can be run without VB and can be copied to another machine and run in the new location. This is possible because the Publish Wizard turns the program that you have written into an executable file, which can be started by the user clicking on an icon on the computer's start menu.

It's worth completing this stage in the development of the project even if you haven't managed to complete all of the programming, because it shows you how a program is made suitable for installation on the computer's hard drive. It is satisfying to see something you have made launch from a start menu, just as professionally produced programs do.

Step 1: launch the publish wizard

45 Click the **Build** icon on the standard toolbar.

Figure 3.31

46 Select **Publish FruitMachine** from the drop-down menu.

The **Publish Wizard** loads:

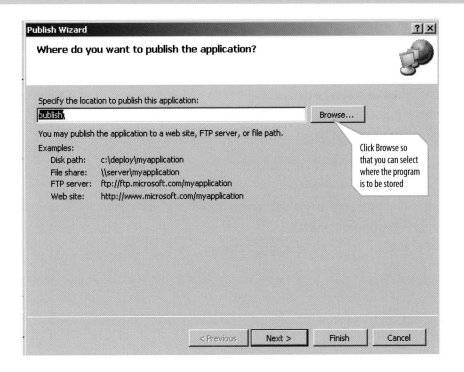

Figure 3.32

Step 2: identify a folder where the published program is to be stored

Click the **Browse** button, which loads the **Open Web Site** dialogue box:

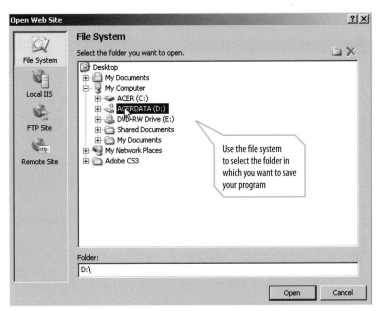

Figure 3.33

 Click **Open**.

You are returned to the **Publish Wizard**.

 Click **Next**.

Step 3: decide on the type of installation

Choose the **CD-ROM** option.

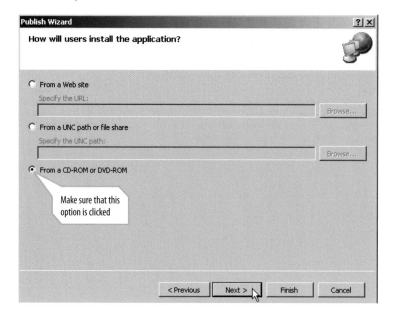

Figure 3.34

 Click **Next**.

Step 4: updates?

Your program is not going to automatically check for updates, so make sure the lower option is clicked in the next page of the wizard:

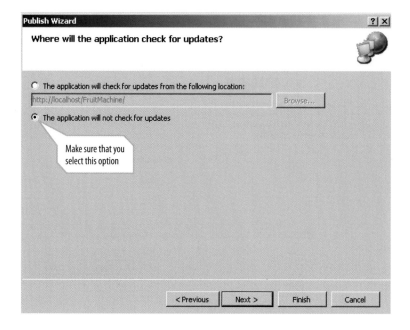

Figure 3.35

 Click **Next**.

Step 5: publish

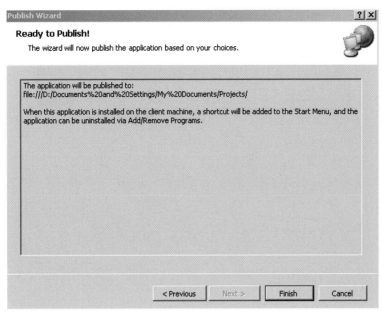

Figure 3.36

 Click **Finish**.

Step 6: install the program

 Give the computer a few minutes to do its stuff then have a look in the folder that you specified in Step 2 for the **Setup** icon:

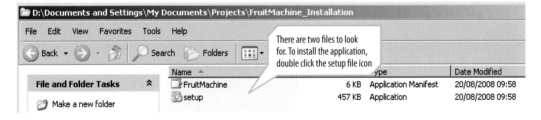

Figure 3.37

 Find the setup file and double click its icon.

The installation starts:

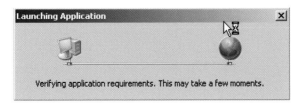

Figure 3.38

The wizard adds a shortcut to the program from the computer's **Start** menu, which is useful.

Figure 3.39

 Test launching the program from the start menu.

 Test the program by asking a friend to play the game.

 Make any changes necessary and then re-publish the project.

That's it!

GET AHEAD

You will want to look through the Tasks to prepare yourself for the project, but here are a few ideas for improving the program:

 Change the images.

 Change the number of images.

 Make the winning message flash on and off by using a For… To… Next loop.

 Provide a text box that shows a total cost for the number of turns selected by the player.

ASSESSMENT POINT

Now let's assess the work. Look back at the table at the beginning of this section (**Target point**) and decide on which of the statements you can answer 'Yes' to.

Did you do as well as you expected? Could you improve your work? Use Word to write a comment to show what you could do to improve your work and remember this when starting your next ICT project.

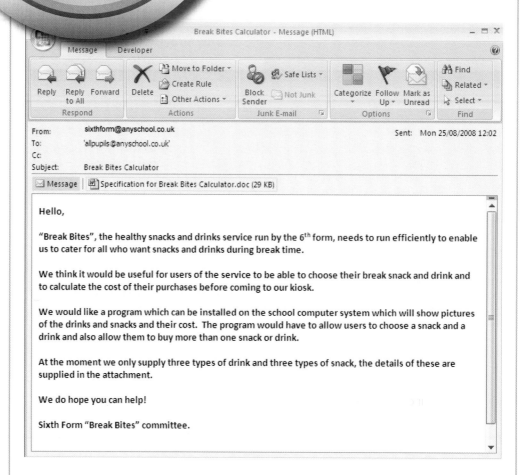

Break Bites Calculator - Message (HTML)

Message   Developer

Reply Reply Forward   Delete   Move to Folder   Block Not Junk   Categorize Follow Mark as   Find
       to All   Create Rule   Sender   Up   Unread   Related
                                  Other Actions   Select
Respond   Actions   Junk E-mail   Options   Find

From: sixthform@anyschool.co.uk   Sent: Mon 25/08/2008 12:02
To: 'allpupils@anyschool.co.uk'
Cc:
Subject: Break Bites Calculator

Message   Specification for Break Bites Calculator.doc (29 KB)

Hello,

"Break Bites", the healthy snacks and drinks service run by the 6th form, needs to run efficiently to enable us to cater for all who want snacks and drinks during break time.

We think it would be useful for users of the service to be able to choose their break snack and drink and to calculate the cost of their purchases before coming to our kiosk.

We would like a program which can be installed on the school computer system which will show pictures of the drinks and snacks and their cost. The program would have to allow users to choose a snack and a drink and also allow them to buy more than one snack or drink.

At the moment we only supply three types of drink and three types of snack, the details of these are supplied in the attachment.

We do hope you can help!

Sixth Form "Break Bites" committee.

Figure Project.1

ASSESSMENT OBJECTIVES

Level 3	Level 4	Level 5	Level 6	Level 7	Level 8
You have made a list of the items need for the Break Bites calculator You have planed the time needed to complete the project	You have broken down tasks (for example, you have made a list of controls or variables that are needed)	You have made a list of the properties of controls and specified the data type for variables and whether they are local or global	You made a clear list of the sequence following pressing the Calculate button		
You have made a plan of the GUI	You have used the properties pane to make some settings	You have set suitable properties for all of the controls	You have made a list of the property settings		
	You have declared a variable	You have successfully assigned a value to a variable	You have written code in the Calculate event handler which is designed to take values from variables	You have written code in the Calculate event handler that calculates a total, either from adding items ordered or from multiplying cost of an item by the setting of a NumericUpDown	You have written code in the Calculate event handler that calculates a total depending on items selected and their number
	You have identified some tests that should be performed	You have made a list of several relevant tests	You have made a list of tests and carried them out	You have carried out tests and, if necessary, rectified any faults	
You have made comments on the effectiveness of your project	You have compared the original specification with the final outcome	You have identified improvements that could be made to your project	You have suggested how improvements could be made to the project	You have identified improvements and related these to users' needs	

The Functional Skills listed below show you the skills you will be demonstrating in your work, but remember you have to know *why* you have chosen to demonstrate them in a particular way and how your choice matches your audience and purpose for the documents.

> Plan what your program is going to do: write a specification for the program based on the information in the email.

> Plan your use of the available time.

❯ Plan the design of the GUI and show what each of the controls is intended to do.

❯ Plan how the program will work, what each control will do and how event handler code is going to be used to make the controls work correctly in the program.

❯ Use VB to design the GUI.

❯ Set the properties of the controls.

❯ Declare variables.

❯ Write event handler code to control the program.

❯ Make sure that the program fits the original specification.

❯ Make sure that the program can be used by the intended users and that they cannot interfere with the program's operation (for example, by ordering an amount of drinks as a word rather than using a number – you will probably solve this by using a NumericUpDown control of course).

❯ Test the program.

❯ Publish the program.

❯ Re-test the published program.

Here's more detail about the project:

The design of the GUI is up to you, but here is an idea that you can use to start your design:

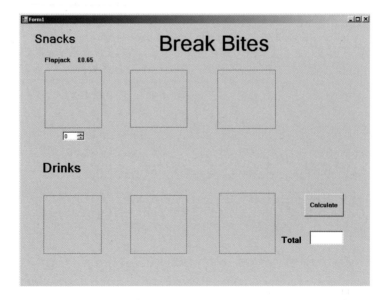

Figure Project.2

The title 'Break Bites', 'Snacks', 'Flapjack' and so on are made using the label control. The idea is that the user sets the NumericUpDown control to whatever number they require for each snack and drink, then presses the Calculate button which shows the total cost in the text box.